Ornament and Object: Canadian Jewellery and Metal Art, 1946–1996

Ornament and Object: Canadian Jewellery and Metal Art, 1946–1996

Anne Barros

The BOSTON
MILLS PRESS

In memory of JB

Published in 1997 by
Boston Mills Press
www.boston-mills.on.ca

Distributed in Canada by
General Distribution Services Inc.
30 Lesmill Road
Toronto, Canada M3B 2T6
Tel 416-445-3333
Fax 416-445-5967
e-mail customer.service@ccmailgw.genpub.com

Distributed in the United States by
General Distribution Services Inc.
85 River Rock Drive, Suite 202
Buffalo, New York 14207
Toll-free 1-800-805-1083
Fax 416-445-5967
e-mail customer.service@ccmailgw.genpub.com

01 00 99 98 97   1 2 3 4 5

Cataloging in Publication Data

Barros, Anne, 1939–
Ornament and object : Canadian jewellery and metal art 1946–1996

Includes bibliographical references and index.
ISBN 1-55046-218-0

1. Art metal-work - Canada - History - 20th century.
2. Jewelry - Canada - History - 20th century. I. Title.

NK6413.A1B37 1997   739'.0971'09045   97-930553-5

Text and cover design by Adams + Associates, Toronto

Editing by James Bosma

Printed in Canada

Contents

Andrew Fussell in his Bloor Street studio, Toronto, early 1940s. Photo courtesy Joan Fussell.

With the recent fiftieth anniversary of the Metal Arts Guild of Ontario, in 1996, it seems an appropriate time to look back on the last five decades of art jewellery and metalwork in Canada. The purpose of this study is to capture something of the postwar studio jewellery movement while many of the key players are alive to tell the story. Although this brief survey is primarily documentation, it is also an attempt to interpret the changing metal scene and place jewellers and their work within a historical context.

The sheer size of this country, and the lack of a national craft publication, have contributed to the relative isolation of Canadian metalsmiths, and to a lack of public awareness of happenings in the field. To begin to remedy this, I have carried out research in the archives of the Metal Arts Guilds of Ontario and Nova Scotia, the Canadian Handicrafts Guild in Montreal, and many provincial craft councils. I also visited seven provinces to conduct personal interviews and visit schools with metal programs. Unfortunately, the paucity of archival information in some provinces, and my limited research budget, have meant that Nova Scotia, Quebec and Ontario are perhaps better represented than other parts of the country. The interpretation of over two hundred questionnaires, completed by contemporary Canadian metalsmiths, rounded out my research.

I have been a silversmith for the past fifteen years, and my point of view — with attention to process and materials as well as to design and societal influences — emerges from within the metalsmithing community. I have organized events by decades; however, often the circumstances that led to the making of specific pieces during the last five decades defy such divisions.

This study includes art jewellery and metal art — ornament and object. To me, "art jewellery" is ornament for the body that shows originality, uniqueness and personal expression. It often explores materials and techniques in new ways, and it sometimes contains historical references and social commentary. "Metal art," which includes hollowware, flatware and sculptural items (and sometimes work in enamel), shares these attributes. But it is indistinct boundaries that bring excitement to this field, which comprises a wide range of making, from the conceptual to the fashion-driven.

I intend to pursue several themes in Canadian metalsmithing, namely, how juried and curated shows have represented the changing metal scene, how metalcraft has been influenced by the design and art worlds, how metalcraft has been affected by the market, and how metalcraft reflects an image of this country.

For reference, I have included a compendium of metalsmiths, with trademarks and biographical information. To aid readers less familiar with metals and techniques, I have included a glossary of terms. A CD-ROM with photographs of the work of over two hundred Canadian metalsmiths is also available from the Metal Arts Guild, Toronto, Ontario.

It is my hope that this book will lead to further documentation of the studio jewellery movement in Canada and its place in our cultural history. I also hope that it will help Canada's jewellers and metalsmiths, and Canadians in general, to have a greater connection with their past and with each other.

Acknowledgments

I wish to acknowledge the many organizations and people who have contributed to this project: the Explorations Program of the Canada Council, the Jean A. Chalmers Fund for Craft, Gael Ferris, and the executive of the Metal Arts Guild of Ontario, especially the fundraising committee headed by Aggie Beynon.

I am also grateful to Stephen Inglis, director of research at the Canadian Museum of Civilization, for guidance in the initial gathering of research; Bill McLellan of the Museum of Anthropology, University of British Columbia, for assistance with photographs; the Vancouver Art Gallery, for permission to quote from *Arts of the Raven*; to Harcourt Brace and Company for permission to quote from *Contemporary Jewelry,* by Philip Morton; to the Royal Ontario Museum for permission to use work from its collection; and to George Mashinter and his students at Georgian College in Barrie, Ontario, for compiling a CD-ROM of my research.

The following associations made archival material available to me: the Metal Arts Guilds of Ontario and Nova Scotia; the Canadian Guild of Crafts in Montreal; the Conseil des métiers d'art du Québec; the Crafts Association of British Columbia; the Ontario Crafts Council; the Nova Scotia Designer Crafts Council; the Nova Scotia Centre for Craft and Design; Nova Scotia College of Art and Design; The Ontario College of Art; and Pickering College, Newmarket, Ontario. The Craft Councils of Alberta, Manitoba and Saskatchewan, the Newfoundland and Labrador Crafts Development Association and the Creative Jewellers Guild of British Columbia also kindly provided me with information.

Mary Pocock, Jim and Jane Robson, Beth Alber, Jan Waldorf, David McAleese, Alison Wiggins, Wendy Shingler, Colleen McCallum and Sue Wakefield offered constructive criticism and help with both the questionnaire and the manuscript. James Evans, Sandra Flood, Jean Johnson, Virginia Wright, Sarah Bodine, Gail Crawford, Rosalyn Morrison, Jocelyne Gobeil and Arlene Gehring gave me invaluable advice.

Without Jeremy Jones's excellent photographs of ten years of Metal Arts Guild exhibitions, I would not have dared this pictorial record. Lastly, I wish to thank all the jewellers and metalsmiths and their families who submitted slides and offered ideas and encouragement (as well as contributions of scrap metal) to help make this book a reality.

Metal as Medium

Historically, a person who worked with metals was denoted by the name of the metal plus the suffix *smith* (meaning "one who smites or hits"). In many countries, however, the term *goldsmith* was synonymous with *jeweller,* and referred to anyone who made objects of adornment in precious metals. Others distinguished between the goldsmith as the designer and maker of jewellery, and the jeweller as the merchant who sold it. Traditionally, the silversmith made objects of larger scale than the jeweller or goldsmith, such as vessels and tableware. Today, some silversmiths define themselves as such because their medium is mainly silver. The objects they make extend from hollowware to jewellery. The blanket-term *metalsmith* has become popular in North America because it reflects an egalitarian approach to all metals.

The use of fire for metalwork has traditionally precluded its being a home craft, as children would get underfoot. With its hammers and hot sparks, smithing was considered man's work. In some societies the jeweller and blacksmith lived apart from others, and daughters were not allowed to learn the craft for fear they would later pass its secrets on to their husband's families. But by the mid-twentieth century in North America, few secrets remained hidden; art jewellers shared knowledge readily and were free to work at home or in separate studios.

Although it is possible to do metalwork without ever using fire, most smiths still choose the control the flame gives them over their material. The metalsmith directly torches the metal, teases the solder to flow in the right direction, watches for the metal to achieve the appropriate colour, or heats the metal until it runs fluid.

Self-discipline is needed to master the many aspects of metalworking, and a jeweller who wishes to be well trained may spend from three to seven years (or more) to acquire mastery in such techniques as fabricating, casting, engraving, soldering, stone setting, raising, electroforming, plating, colouring and finishing. Drawing, rendering and photography are also important skills for the contemporary jeweller.

Most jewellers are fastidious and precise in their work, as precious metal demands a careful approach. Unlike clay, which can be worked with relative abandon, precious metals must be cautiously weighed out and watched over, as mistakes can be costly. Tools must be kept in prime condition, and sweepings are carefully sifted and returned to the refiner. For some, these are stultifying aspects of the medium that inhibit creativity.

Modern jewellery and hollowware design are materials based, and many artists are drawn to metal for its toughness, malleability and durability. As Philip Morton, a prominent practitioner and author, wrote in *Contemporary Jewelry*: "a recognition and exploitation of the intrinsic characteristics of materials is fundamental to the ethics of contemporary design." Although much inspiration for jewellery has originated in painting and sculpture, the properties of the metals themselves have also stimulated experimentation. Some metalsmiths even claim that the medium chose them.

1

Fig. 1. Nancy Meek Pocock brooch, late 1940s, sterling silver, fabricated, 7 x 3 cm. Collection: Patricia Dingle.

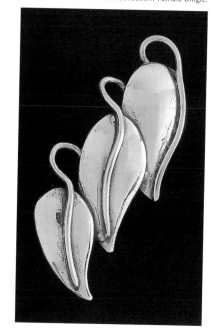

13

Postwar Canada

The Formation of Guilds

In 1948, in response to a request by Ontario's provincial government for metal objects for a craft exhibition, the newly formed Metal Arts Guild (MAG) — a small group of art jewellers and silversmiths — met one evening in Toronto to select pieces. Among the chosen works were a salt-and-pepper set by Douglas Boyd, a place setting by Andrew Fussell, and a floral brooch by Nancy Meek Pocock (Fig. 1). Each of these pieces was sterling silver, and stylistically they were modern, with flowing lines and restrained ornamentation. Boyd and Fussell had learned their craft from a Swedish immigrant, and Meek Pocock was an art-college graduate.

This postwar meeting was representative of occurrences in other North American cities, including Halifax, Vancouver and San Francisco. It signalled a resurgence in craft that encompassed not just metal but also clay, glass, wood and fibre. War and industrialization had taken their toll on metalsmithing, but the arts and craft tradition lingered. During the twenties, thirties and forties, jewellery and metalworking were taught in secondary school shop classes, in some art and teacher-training schools, and by individual smiths (see Fig. 2). But by mid-century there were only about a dozen silversmiths working in Toronto, compared to sixty-nine, recorded a hundred years earlier. Throughout Canada, a small number of amateurs and professionals were attempting to maintain the tradition of handcrafted metal in an era of mass-produced cutlery and jewellery. Their concern for education, design, quality marks and professionalism led them to form metal-art associations.

Fig. 2. Wednesday-afternoon class at Andrew Fussell's home studio, Asquith Street, Toronto, c. 1945.

Fig. 3. Trademark of the Metal Arts Guild of Nova Scotia.

Metal arts guilds — modelled after the English Worshipful Company of Goldsmiths — were established in Ontario, in 1946, and in Nova Scotia, in 1951. Along with encouraging the cultural and commercial development of metal as an art medium, MAG Ontario's plan was to provide instruction, examine proficiency and establish standards. MAG Nova Scotia's prime purpose, as expressed by Morna Anderson, who wrote its history, was to "assist each other . . . and advance members' knowledge in what was a hobby for them." Among its concerns were work standards, prices and marketing, and tool making, as well as proper care of exhibition work and the exchange of ideas and designs.

On the West Coast, the Creative Jewellers Guild of British Columbia was formed in the 1950s to meet the needs of people who created silver and gold jewellery as a hobby. Its goals were to help members improve their skills, learn new techniques, and realize enjoyment from making and designing jewellery. This group provided a much-needed opportunity for amateurs to share skills, as there was little information available to those practicing outside of the profession.

While MAG Nova Scotia and the Creative Jewellers Guild of British Columbia aimed to be organizations for hobbyists, and MAG Ontario welcomed amateur members, the professional ranks were determined to remain separate in order to uphold their high standards. They grew

to dislike the term *handicraft*, as it began to take on a hobbyist connotation. In an era when craft education was supported by provincial governments as a means to supplement family income, use leisure time creatively and provide therapy for returning veterans, dedicated teachers wanted to see better work made.

The founders of MAG Ontario considered their organization to be an antidote to the Ontario branch of the Canadian Handicrafts Guild — a national organization that had begun in Montreal in 1906 and spread to many provinces. The metal guild was more narrowly focussed on the needs of its members than the larger multi-media guild, which, in the view of many craftspeople, was run by well-meaning socialites.

MAG Nova Scotia obtained its own trademark — a crest with a salmon flanked by three mallets, derived from the coat of arms of Edinburgh's Guild of Hammermen — in 1953 (Fig. 3). In the centuries-old tradition of British hallmarking, this mark enabled the guild to assay and assure the quality of precious metals in its members' work. The Canadian Precious Metals Marking Act (still in effect) held the maker liable for the marking of precious metal. It did not, however, provide an assay office where work could be tested and stamped before sale. MAG Nova Scotia was the only Canadian guild so seriously dedicated to precious metal standards that it expended the time and effort to stamp its members' work.

14

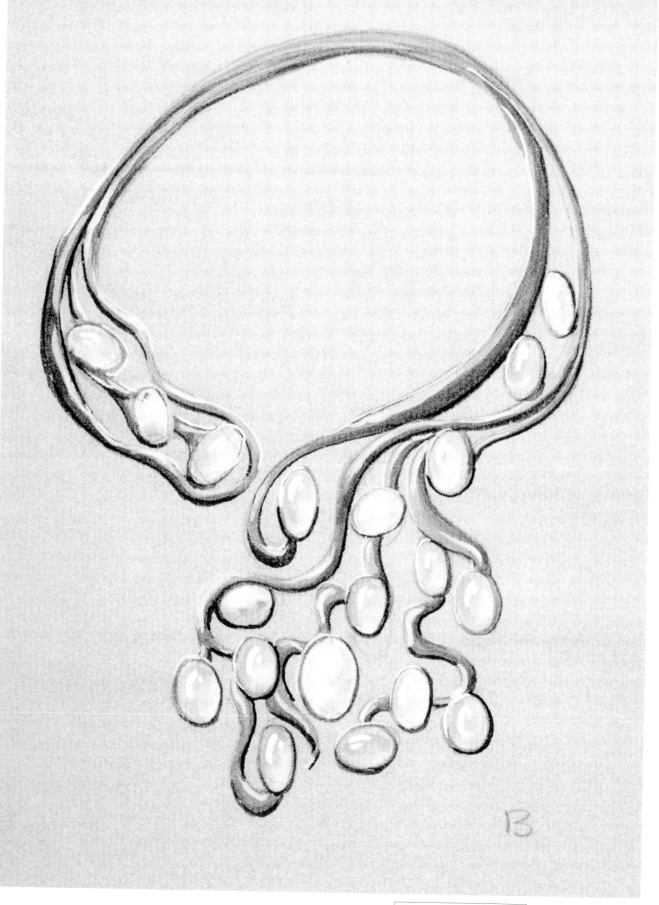

Fig. 4. Nancy Meek Pocock rendering for neckpiece, 1940s.

Early Canadian Metal Artists

Art jewellery and silversmithing benefited from the postwar establishment of metal and jewellery guilds in Canada. Guilds made it possible for skills to be passed on from teachers and professionals to students and dedicated hobbyists. They also strove to uphold standards in precious metal marking and workmanship, and to educate the public about what to look for in handmade metalwork. But, in keeping with the tradition of guilds in England and Western Europe, discussions at meetings often centred more on such practical issues as pay rates for metal instructors and how to properly display work than on art theory or aesthetics. In calling them "art guilds," however, members were asserting their conviction that metal was a material for artistic expression.

Conscious of the possibilities of metal for personal and artistic expression, pioneers in the Canadian art jewellery movement began laying the groundwork for its postwar direction. Nancy Meek Pocock was one of the founding directors of MAG Ontario (and the only one to be described as a "silversmith" in the guild's letters patent). After graduating from the Ontario College of Art (OCA) in 1930, Pocock studied design and bench-work for a year in Paris. Her drawings, with their scrolling floral motifs, reveal the influence of the French approach to decorative art (see Fig. 4). She developed her own style using flowers, leaves and stones to express "beauty, harmony and peace." Clients brought her loose stones to be set in her "modern way" — an artistic approach that eschewed the refinement of commercial jewellery.

During the thirties and forties, local artists would gather at her small studio in the Gerrard Village section of Toronto to discuss ideas over a glass of wine. Later, with her husband, John Pocock, she moved to Yorkville, where both continued to work until 1970.

Another Toronto-area smith, Swedish-born Hokan Rudolph (Rudy) Renzius, began metalsmithing in his father's coppersmith shop. He later studied at the Malmo Technical University in Sweden; under Just Anderson, in Copenhagen; and under Adolf von Mayerhofer, in Munich. Working mainly in pewter, Renzius designed a wide range of objects, from coffee and tea sets to jewellery. His well-planished volumetric forms were neatly fabricated and inviting to use (for an example, see Fig. 5). A 1929 exhibition of interiors at New York's Metropolitan Museum of Art featured a dressing table set designed and made by him. Before the Second World War, Renzius gave classes in metalsmithing to Andrew Fussell, Harold Gordon Stacey and most probably to Douglas Boyd. Because of this he is credited with launching the first generation of contemporary Toronto smiths. From 1935 to 1960, he taught arts and crafts at Pickering College, in Newmarket, Ontario. Renzius's Swedish metalsmithing influences, from his careful raising of forms to his broad philosophy of artistic integrity, had a significant effect on Southern Ontario metalwork, and, as a result, the area exhibited a strength in hollowware in national exhibitions from the 1930s through the 1950s.

Andrew Fussell emigrated to Canada from England in 1926 and became a popular teacher and maker. He took metalsmithing classes with Renzius from 1930 to 1932, and studied architectural drawing and sculpture at Toronto's Central Technical School, where he later taught. Like many industrious smiths of his time, Fussell acknowledged being largely self-taught. His studio, a magpie's haven of equipment and tools in seeming disarray, was always open for students to stop by to purchase a bit of silver or use a tool. In design, Fussell looked to natural forms, as represented in his use of wildflowers on spoon handles and brooches. But the influence of Renzius was clearly evident in his early hollowware, with its rounded forms (see Fig. 6). Fussell went on to develop his own style, tackling very large planished hollowware pieces, some two feet in diameter, and unusual oblong bowl shapes, such as the one that won him the best-in-show at MAG Ontario's 1959 exhibition.

Fig. 6.   Andrew Fussell   pewter tea set, late 1930s. Photo: Ashley & Crippen.

Fig. 7. Douglas Boyd Box presented to Princess Elizabeth and the Duke of Edinburgh, 1951, sterling silver, 12 x 12 x 3.5 cm.

Fig. 8. Harold G. Stacey raised bowl, 1949, sterling silver. Purchased by U.S. Department of State. Exhibited at Metropolitan Museum of Art, New York City. Photo: Peter Croydon.

Douglas Boyd embraced metal as a hobby in the 1930s and, by 1937, was winning prizes for hollowware at the Canadian National Exhibition (CNE). Mostly self-taught, Boyd had a flair for design and marketing. "It is high time the world knows that we Canadians do more than raise mink here," he declared. Much of his work was commissioned, including the chalice presented to the new Coventry Cathedral in England on behalf of the Province of Ontario and its craftspeople. For the visit of Princess Elizabeth and the Duke of Edinburgh, in 1951, Boyd made a sterling silver cigarette box (Fig. 7). He acknowledged to the *Daily Times Gazette* of Oshawa that, given just two-and-a-half-days' notice, "the design had perforce to be simple." He also wanted "something that would express Canada — full, strong and clean." With sloping sides reminiscent of a corn crib, and a trillium knob (Ontario's floral symbol), the piece succeeded as a Canadian expression in metal. As an active member of MAG Ontario, Boyd was president in 1949–50 and won the Steel Trophy for best-in-show in 1957.

On MAG Ontario's founding document, Harold Gordon Stacey described himself as an "Instructor Craftsman," but to others he was known as "Canada's silversmith." In 1950, Stacey was chosen by Steuben Glass to head a two-year experimental workshop in New York for the design and fabrication of silver articles. This appointment was a tribute to Stacey's pre-eminent craftsmanship.

From 1947 to 1951, a series of Silversmithing Workshop Conferences, begun by Margret Craver and sponsored by Handy and Harman Precious Metal Refiners, was held at the Rhode Island School of Design, in Providence, Rhode Island, and at the School for American Craftsmen, in Rochester, New York. These conferences have been credited with passing on the techniques of raising and embellishing to a new generation of studio craftsmen. Baron Erik Fleming, Court Silversmith to His Majesty the King of Sweden, was Harold Stacey's instructor at one of these, and Stacey later claimed that he learned more about silversmithing from Baron Fleming than from anyone else before or after.

Stacey learned Fleming's method of raising, which involved stretching the silver from a very thick, small disc. In this method, the disc is hammered outward from the centre and, as it becomes thinner, it is formed upward, retaining substantial thickness in the outside edge. Stacey used this technique for the bowl he displayed at the Metropolitan Museum of Art in 1949 (Fig. 8). Following these workshops, in her review of the exhibition that appeared in *Craft Horizons*, Virginia Wireman Cute, director of silversmithing and jewelry at the Philadelphia Museum School of Art, wrote: "… my thumb and forefinger itch to lift the cover of Harold Stacey's covered bowl." Smoothly hammered metal surfaces were a regular attribute of Stacey's hand-formed pieces, which he continued to produce until his death in 1979.

MAG Nova Scotia began with seventeen charter members. The members benefited from the technical expertise of Clifford Brown, who offered engraving classes. Brown, the Halifax guild's warden, and a silversmith for thirty-one years, was associated with Henry Birks and Sons. In 1939, for a gold maple leaf, Brown was given permission to use the Royal Coat of Arms and the inscription "By Appointment, Jeweller to Queen Elizabeth."

There was a strong Scottish influence in the work of members of MAG Nova Scotia. Many designs included thistle patterns, often combined with native agates. For example, in 1967, Mr. and Mrs. Norman Anderson, of Halifax, designed and made a sterling silver kilt pin (Fig. 9) for Her Majesty Queen Elizabeth, the Queen Mother. The pin featured an agate from Scots Bay on the Bay of Fundy, with a thistle above it. The blade was engraved with maple leaves and Nova Scotia mayflowers.

Donald Cameron MacKay, Principal of the Nova Scotia College of Art and Design (NSCAD) from 1945 to 1970, was an honorary member of MAG Nova Scotia. Considered a leading connoisseur and collector of silver, MacKay had a great interest in early Nova Scotia silversmiths.

19

Fig. 9. Mr. and Mrs. Norman Anderson design for kilt pin with cut and polished agate. Presented to Her Majesty Queen Elizabeth the Queen Mother on the occasion of her opening of the annual Highland Games at Antigonish, Nova Scotia, July 1967.

He edited *Master Goldsmiths and Silversmiths of Nova Scotia,* a book that documented the province's fine metalworking tradition. He also designed work for members of MAG to create as presentation pieces. At NSCAD, MacKay promoted day and evening courses in silversmithing.

Henry Birks, head of Canada's leading jewellery store chain, was an important patron to both MAG Nova Scotia and MAG Ontario. In Toronto he contributed toward exhibition awards, and in Halifax he established the Birks Medal for design. The skilled craftsmen employed by Henry Birks and Sons also shared their knowledge in workshops and meetings.

Few studio jewellers in the postwar era had proper shops or sizable clienteles, and most designer-craftspeople operated small studios in their homes and earned very modest incomes from their work unless they could secure permanent teaching or industry jobs. Harold Stacey's son remembers the noise: "bangbang-*bang*, bangbang-*bang*, a rarely varying tattoo that penetrated the first and second storeys filled the walls with steady metallic ringing [and] echoed in sleep long after the barrage had ceased in the small hours of the morning."

Some jewellers, including Nancy Meek Pocock, chose small shops with modest rents in bohemian sections of town as places to work and sell. They would also send work to local craft outlets and teach on the side. A modest entrepreneurial venture combined with a simple lifestyle dedicated to handwork exemplified the studio craft movement.

Silversmith Carl Poul Petersen, of Montreal, had a different approach. Danish born, Petersen had apprenticed under Georg Jensen and Kastor Hansen at the Georg Jensen Silversmithy in Copenhagen, the most significant postwar design influence for metal. The Jensen firm produced silverware using a combination of hand raising and planishing, and commercial manufacturing techniques including spinning. High-quality workmanship was wedded to a design aesthetic born of Art Nouveau and Scandinavian natural forms. Jensen designers changed over the years, but the firm continued to be known for its clean, flowing lines and liquid forms.

Petersen's work was well received in Canada, where the Scandinavian look was being popularized in magazine articles, lectures and workshops. By 1947, according to the research of Gloria Lesser, of Montreal, Petersen headed a firm that employed more than twenty silversmiths (including his three sons), many of whom he had trained as apprentices. In response to demand from both the United States and Canada for his finely crafted hollowware and jewellery, Petersen was purchasing four tons of silver annually. Among the firm's specialties were Jewish ritual pieces, wedding gifts and presentation pieces. Standardized shapes and patterns in flatware and tableware underscored an emphasis on quality production over innovation. Petersen pieces displayed an organic approach to design, with applied floral motifs and beaded ornamentation (see Fig. 10). This synthesis of craft technique and industrial methods lasted until the firm closed in 1979, after Nelson Bunker Hunt's dealings in the silver market forced prices to rise dramatically.

Jewellery and hollowware were featured in multimedia craft exhibitions held by the Canadian Handicrafts Guild, in Montreal, and by the CNE, in Toronto. Because the CNE was a national venue and its awards for the best jewellery and hollowware were often accompanied by gifts of precious metal from refiners, it was highly regarded. The CNE and large national department stores, including Eaton's and Simpson's, also provided venues for craft organizations to present demonstrations to the public. These demonstrations, often numbering thousands in attendance, sometimes led to sales, but more importantly, stimulated public interest in metalwork.

Although the numbers of craftspeople involved in metalwork never equalled those in ceramics or fibre, the small group of participants proved as resolute as their medium. Their activism helped sow the seeds for later exhibitions and grants.

In 1949, members of MAG Ontario contributed a brief, entitled "The Metal Artist in Canada," to the Massey Commission (the Royal Commission on National Development in the Arts, Letters and Sciences). As a young nation of about twelve million people inhabiting the second largest country of the world, Canada emerged from the Second World War with a sense of national pride. Artists were excited about their work. But the Canadian public was still largely indifferent to artistic achievement. It was the hope of the Massey Commission that art, like oil and ore, might become an exciting and exportable national resource and that spending on the arts would become a wise economic investment.

The Massey Report recommended that the federal government establish scholarships, grants and other financial inducements to encourage Canadian culture. Ultimately, this led to the establishment of the Canada Council. Few gold and silversmiths would receive grants from the Canada Council, which aimed at promoting fine art, not craft. They would, however, be supported by the subsequent establishment of provincial arts councils.

Fig. 10. | C a r l P o u l P e t e r s e n | Corn pattern covered dish, 1954, sterling silver, spun bottom, fabricated and planished top, 9 x 13.5 cm. Photo: Jeremy Jones.

Fig. 11. Harold G. Stacey coffee pot, 1950, sterling silver with rosewood handle, 21 cm. high. Photo: Jeremy Jones.

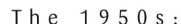

2

The 1950s:

Modernism and Metal

In the summer 1950 edition of *Canadian Art,* Andrew Bell reviewed the *Exhibition of Contemporary Canadian Arts,* which celebrated the fiftieth anniversary of the Toronto Art Gallery. The exhibition boasted 816 pieces, from paintings and graphic art to architecture and crafts, including some metalwork.

In his review, Bell offered harsh criticisms of the Canadian art scene, referring to Canadians as "inhibited," and "disciples of gentle compromise." He put forward this challenge: "if our artists are to do their best work, some of them must struggle to free themselves of these limiting national characteristics." He called the exhibition a "depressing expression of our national reserve" and asserted that "our crafts tend too much to be a meaningless reproduction of what used to go on in Europe." He added that our artists "lack ... faith in themselves and a vision of what honest thinking and imagination can achieve." Not even the layman was blameless: "We still think of our artists as luxuries, and deny them scandalously the adrenalin of basic encouragement."

Bell's review was illustrated with a sterling silver coffee pot by Harold Stacey (Fig. 11). Stacey's piece had some of the merits Bell was searching for: clear form and a modern functional presence. It did not duplicate past European style but was a modernist expression that found its inspiration in Scandinavian silversmithing.

But the austerity of modernism was not yet popular with the majority of the Canadian public, who still preferred traditional forms and materials. In an effort to educate people about modern designs, the National Film Board and the newly created National Industrial Design Council collaborated on a short film called *Designed for Living*. In retrospect, the documentary is a good example of postwar propaganda. A narrator comments on a modern chair: "Lovely, isn't it? And so is the future." Of course, the government's promotion of modernism had little to do with aesthetics: Canadian industry needed a market for the products of its retooled factories.

Coming to terms with modernism was sometimes difficult for the metalsmith too. The modernist desire for a rupture with the past was antithetical to the craft's reliance on tradition, and modernism's "peculiar dislike for the hand," as John Bentley Mays put it, was at odds with the metalsmith's love for handling and shaping materials. Because modernism favoured the machine over the hand, metalsmiths began to worry that they would lag behind in contemporary design. The metalsmith often had to fight against hard-learned skills — to fabricate pieces with a machine-made look — in order to be accepted within the modern aesthetic. As Muriel Rose explained in *Canadian Art*, "the metalwork self-consciously displays its hammer marks, and the more sophisticated purchaser prefers to leave such things in the shop." During the Arts and Crafts Movement, the planished finish had been integral to the look of the work, as it was with some Scandinavian modern silver. In the forties and fifties, however, it became associated with poor-quality work cheaply turned out for the souvenir market.

Stacey's coffee pot displayed an exquisitely planished finish on a constructed form. With its long, straight lines, the piece could have been machine made. The design, as he explained to *Mayfair* in 1951, "developed from the idea of combining a circular base with a diamond-shaped opening, chiefly because the point of the diamond makes for dripless pouring." Stacey cared about function and wanted an avant-garde look, but he chose to leave the markings of the hammer, which fragment the light that hits the surface and counteract the machined look. In such a way, many smiths showed a modern influence while ignoring some aspects of the movement. It took a great deal of technical skill to create the modernist aesthetic in metal. Instead of raising forms from metal discs, which was difficult enough, modern design often demanded that flat sheets of metal be fabricated in very angular ways, soldered together without warping, and then highly polished. Most silversmiths wanted to do modern work, so they stretched their skills to accommodate. Some later turned to the lathe and rivets, while others made forms no machine could possibly duplicate.

For the jeweller who had been introduced to metalwork in an art environment, mastery of technique was often secondary to personal expression. Influenced by modern painting and sculpture, the emphasis in art school was more on innovation and the creative use of materials than on technical perfection. Technique was best taught at provincial trade schools, where a "project" approach to teaching was used. Students would invariably begin by having to make a square box of set dimensions and graduate to a "gents" ring with set stone. Art schools reacted against the sterile perfection of most trade jewellery, with its cluster rings and boring brooches, and the art student spent a great deal of time learning drawing and design. As Philip Morton wrote in his ground-breaking book, *Contemporary Jewelry*, "honest treatment of materials is more important than refinement of craftsmanship."

Although modernism espoused a functional simplicity, it encompassed many different styles — curvilinear, rectilinear, avant-garde and retrospective. Thus many jewellers and silversmiths felt their work fit within the modernist canon, although there was great visual diversity. While other metalsmiths remained decidedly conservative, prodding reviews like Andrew Bell's, along with workshops and exhibitions in Scandinavian modern design, helped promote the spare modern aesthetic among Canadian smiths.

Fig. 12. ┃ Hero Kielman ┃ teapot, 1960, sterling silver, rosewood, 12 x 22 cm.

European Master Jewellers

The development of Canadian art jewellery is greatly indebted to the arrival in Canada of a number of master jewellers from Europe. Many came over in the 1950s; others had come earlier but it took postwar prosperity for them to make their mark.

Hero Kielman arrived in Canada in 1953 from the Netherlands. He had a diploma in gold and silversmithing from the Dutch Governmental School of Arts and Crafts, in Schoonhoven, and experience with his own jewellery business in The Hague. He found the conservative environment of Toronto an enormous change from the more cosmopolitan atmosphere of Europe: "Imagine drawing the curtains on department-store windows on Sunday in order not to violate the Sabbath."

This was the age of rhinestone jewellery and porcelain figurines. Luxury goods in other than traditional wares were not available or even demanded. Jewellery stores across Canada carried a time-honoured line of goods, including mostly Neoclassical and Rococo silverware. But often, as in St. John's and Halifax, important pieces of jewellery or hollowware were ordered from England rather than commissioned locally.

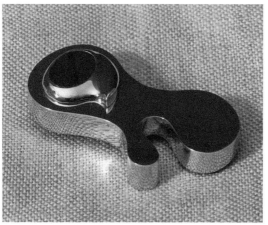

Fig. 13. | Georges Delrue | brooch, 1945, gold, lapis lazuli.

Fig. 14. | Georges Delrue | brooch, 1945, gold, amethyst.

Kielman soon began to teach at the Provincial Institute of Trades in Toronto. Looking across Canada, he saw his School of Jewellery Arts as the only program offering complete instruction in jewellery. *Canadian Jeweller* magazine, in 1959, reported that the school covered diamond setting, jewellery repair, casting, model making, electroplating, the use of hand tools and machines, polishing, and finishing, in addition to detailed studies of gems and precious metals. Pressure from the commercial jewellery community for trained workers, especially setters, was the stimulus for beginning the program, which offered a two-year diploma with a third-year option for specialization. After the Second World War, casting with the aid of rubber molds became the main method of jewellery manufacture. This created a demand for model makers and less-skilled workers. Although most Institute students were oriented toward the jewellery industry, there were some hobbyists. Many of these recreational jewellers were very dedicated and did fine work.

Kielman's own jewellery had a dramatic thrust to it. As his renderings demonstrate [Plate 1 (for plates, see colour insert)], coloured stones were suspended some distance from the shank of his rings, and flowing curves made the rings easy to slip over the fingers. In his hollowware, Kielman preferred unusual forms, which were not as easily raised as round forms and certainly could not have been machine spun. His 1960 teapot (Fig. 12), a sturdy, oblong form with a sunken top and merging handle, possesses a rhythmic unity; its expert craftsmanship and solidity are testimony to Kielman's Dutch background and training.

Montreal, with its French flare and vibrant art community, was the most cosmopolitan of Canadian cities in the 1950s. The École du Meuble trained students in furniture making, ceramics and interior decoration. Paul-Émile Borduas, Quebec's pre-eminent abstract painter, had taught there and left his mark on the school. Paul Beau, a native Montrealer and one of Canada's foremost metal craftsmen, executed small objects in the spirit of the Arts and Crafts Movement and also had many architectural commissions. With a history of wood sculpture and ecclesiastical wares in metal dating to its early settlement, the province of Quebec embraced the decorative arts.

Gabriel Lucas headed an atelier in Montreal that attracted such European jewellers as Georges Schwartz, Hans Gehrig, Walter Schluep and Georges Delrue. According to Robert Ayre, Delrue, a native of France, wanted to "create something in jewellery corresponding to what [was] being done in painting and sculpture." Stimulated by his friendship with Canadian sculptor Louis Archambault, and by the work of European artists Arp, Miró and Lipchitz, Delrue produced flat, hollow, gold brooches in biomorphic shapes (Figs. 13 + 14). Large, set stones were a lively contrast to the protozoan metal forms, and the deeply curved edges created strong negative spaces. Delrue also used simple structural motifs of opposing constructed lines, and made focal points of bezel-set agates. This work was not unlike that of Delrue's contemporaries in American studio jewellery. Delrue insisted, "Let us be contemporary .... If we are really honest we will be true to the spirit of our own time." Many jewellers and metalsmiths in other cities shared Delrue's philosophy but found it difficult to make a living selling modern metal pieces to the public.

Jewellers Pius Kaufman, from Switzerland, and Thomas Primavesi, from Austria, met in Montreal and established a business there in 1954. Primavesi's family owned the Wiener Werkstatte — a society of artists and craftspeople founded and directed by Dr. Josef Hoffmann — from 1903 to 1932. With European training, and attention to modern design, these two men took a three-dimensional, sculptural approach to jewellery, a tradition that continues in Quebec jewellery.

Appreciation for contemporary design came more readily in the dramatic West Coast setting of Vancouver, and the city became the centre of modernism in Canada. According to Charles H. Scott, the "'outside-inside' and 'inside-outside' mode of architecture" was "rapidly eating up the fringe of forest that ... circled the city."

In 1952, Karl Stittgen arrived from Germany as a finemechanic (watch and clockmaker) and soon found himself teaching enamelling and co-founding a craft gallery, Creative Hands, in Vancouver. Feeling that most jewellery stores were too diversified with non-jewellery items such as china, crystal, cameras and luggage, Stittgen created a setting that included high-quality Canadian ceramics as a background for his own work. He began sketching one-of-a-kind designs for Canadian women who had been more accustomed to buying costume jewellery. His philosophy held that a piece of jewellery should say something about its maker as well as its wearer — a truly modernist sentiment. A good example of his work — and collage technique — is a pendant entitled *Harmoni Mundi* (Plate 2), which incorporates a watch face, a classical profile, and gemstones including the favoured western Canadian ammonite. Stittgen introduced the concept of jewellery

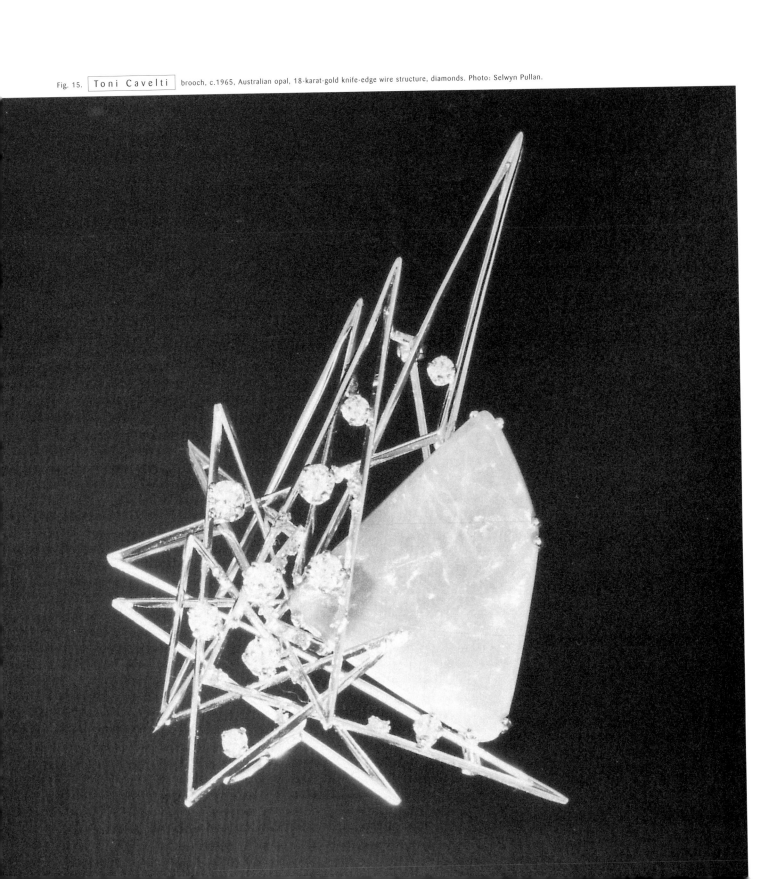

as "wearable art" to what became a loyal clientele, and his design and business skills have made him an important force in British Columbia jewellery. In 1961 he started the first of a series of galleries — named Gold and Silver — that spread to Calgary and San Francisco, and in 1965 he started an apprenticeship program for goldsmiths. The exhibition *Trends and Traditions,* at the Cartwright Gallery in Vancouver, was curated by Stittgen in 1987 to draw attention to the innovative work of western Canadian goldsmiths.

Vancouver also became home to Toni Cavelti, who arrived from his native Switzerland in 1954. Although he recalls being told that he was overqualified and that he should have stayed in Europe, Cavelti persisted and soon began winning international awards for his diamond jewellery. His approach was both architectural and contemporary. An example of this is a brooch he created to hold a massive Australian opal with an uneven angular shape (Fig. 15). The piece is an abstract construction of tightly controlled gold wires studded with diamonds and suggests a carefully orchestrated outburst of energy.

In Winnipeg, German-born Ludwig Nickel came to Canada in 1956 after training at the Benedictine Monastery of Muensterschwarzach under master goldsmith and enamellist Adelman Doelger. Nickel specialized in liturgical work. His chalices, crosses and tabernacles can be seen at St. Paul's College at the University of Manitoba, and in churches across Canada. When the liturgical changes of Vatican II caused a decline in ecclesiastical commissions, Nickel concentrated more on jewellery. In 1972, he opened a design studio in Winnipeg, where he continued to experiment with enamels. He liked bold geometric forms against strong background colours, and he achieved incredible colour results in his small-scale work — which included boxes and rings (see Plate 3, colour insert) — and in his larger wall panels. Nickel worked under the protection of his workshop Madonna until his death in 1989.

Native Design

The best examples of metal design by Canada's indigenous people are found in the work of Bill Reid and other West Coast Native artists. In 1948, Reid, while working for the CBC, enrolled in a jewellery night class at Ryerson Institute of Technology, in downtown Toronto. He told his instructor, James Green, that he wanted to make "some articles with Indian motifs." Green, born and trained in Britain, found Reid singularly adept and took him very seriously.

Reid's maternal grandfather was the last of a line of Haida Indian silversmiths, and, with some training, he hoped to carry on the family tradition. Although he designed and made some contemporary jewellery, including two complex neckpieces, Reid is best known for his work inspired by Haida forms. French anthropologist Claude Levi-Strauss credits Reid with bringing Northwest Coast art "into a dialogue with the whole of mankind." Reid, who today considers himself as primarily a goldsmith, began that dialogue by "shamelessly copying" in order to understand the dynamics of Haida art. It is an art rich with animal figures represented from the front, side, inside and outside, almost to the point of abstraction (see Fig. 16). As Reid explained in *Arts of the Raven*:

> The basic lines of a box design start with a major image, rush to the limits of the field, turn back on themselves, are pushed and squeezed towards the centre, and rippling over and around the internal patterns, start the motion again. Where form touches form, the line is compressed, and the tension almost reaches the breaking point, before it is released in another broad flowing curve .... All is containment and control, and yet always there seems to be an effort to escape.

Soon Reid was no longer merely copying his rich history, but creatively interpreting it. He employed the goldsmithing techniques of chasing and repoussé to create more three-dimensional figures (see Plate 4), which he sometimes inlaid with ivory and abalone. He later carved and cast fully three-dimensional figures of ravens, frogs and eagles. His castings grew larger, culminating in his monumental sculpture *Spirit of Haida Gwaii,* which now sits before the Canadian Embassy in Washington, D.C. For his fine craftsmanship and use of traditional images, Reid is credited with stimulating a renaissance in Northwest Coast Indian art. As a goldsmith, Reid is part of both Haida and English-Canadian traditions. In a long list of honours, he received the Saidye Bronfman Award for Excellence in the Crafts in 1986.

First National Fine Crafts Exhibition

In June 1957, the National Gallery of Canada staged its *First National Fine Crafts Exhibition* as a record of craft work at the time. It was an invitational show in which both jewellery and hollowware were well represented. Among the jurors was the Gallery's Associate Director, D. W. Buchanan, and an American designer, John Van Koert, who had also been a member of the jury for the influential *Designer-Craftsmen USA Exhibition*, which had come to the Royal Ontario Museum in 1955. The jurors noted that they were not necessarily looking for Canadian motifs in the work submitted. If anything, there was a healthy reaction against maple leaves and beavers. They found the average level of design in the crafts in Canada to be rising, but indicated that "true excellence [was] still only to be found among a few of our most supremely gifted workers." The craft component for the Canadian Pavilion in the *Universal and International Exhibition* in Brussels, in 1958, was chosen from this exhibition. Among the chosen metalwork was jewellery by Maurice Brault, Pius Kaufman, Thomas Primavesi, Georges Delrue, Nancy Meek Pocock, Helga Palko, Bill Reid and Harold and Winnifred Fox; hollowware by Gilles Beaugrand, Douglas Boyd, Lois Etherington Betteridge and C.P. Petersen; and enamel by Françoise Desrochers-Drolet and Monique Drolet-Côté.

The jewellery of Meek Pocock, Palko, Delrue, and Cavelti, although distinctly different, was all influenced by modern art. In general, it was beautiful ornament and was made to be worn. Their work was also well designed, exemplified by lines, angles and planes, and often featuring focal points of gemstones. The hollowware of Stacey, Boyd, Fussell, Kielman and Petersen showed a similar design-oriented approach. Function dictated form and there was no decoration. The strength of the Scandinavian modern tradition — Renzius and Stacey had studied under Swedish masters, and Petersen under a Danish master — was clear. In contrast, the jewellery and hollowware of Bill Reid, with its Haida imagery, was not only beautiful ornament, but, in a modernist world of clean surfaces, it boldly displayed total surface embellishment.

Enamelling in Quebec reached its apex during the 1950s. Marcel Dupond, a French painter and enamellist who emigrated to Quebec in 1946, is credited with being the precursor of the modern enamelling movement there. The École des Beaux-Arts de Québec integrated enamel into its fine-arts curriculum, and enamels took many prizes in the decorative arts category in provincial competitions. The work most often appeared in flat plaque format, in which the artist used enamel as a colour medium for drawings influenced by nature or for semi-abstract representations of the human figure.

By the end of the 1950s, when, according to historian Desmond Morton, "most Canadians did not seem to care," the federal government began to encourage and subsidize the arts. The talents of many European jewellers had been absorbed, and those jewellers were now developing markets for their work and taking on apprentices to pass on their expertise. The end of the decade also saw the beginnings of a revival of a rich Native tradition on the West Coast and the peak of a vibrant enamelling movement in Quebec. Against this backdrop, the modernist aesthetic, with its simplified forms and restrained ornamentation, was slowly winning converts from the entrenched aesthetics of traditional French and English metalwork.

Fig. 16. Bill Reid box with lid, 1964, sterling silver, 10 x 9 x 8.8 cm. Photo: Bill McLennan, University of British Columbia Museum of Anthropology.

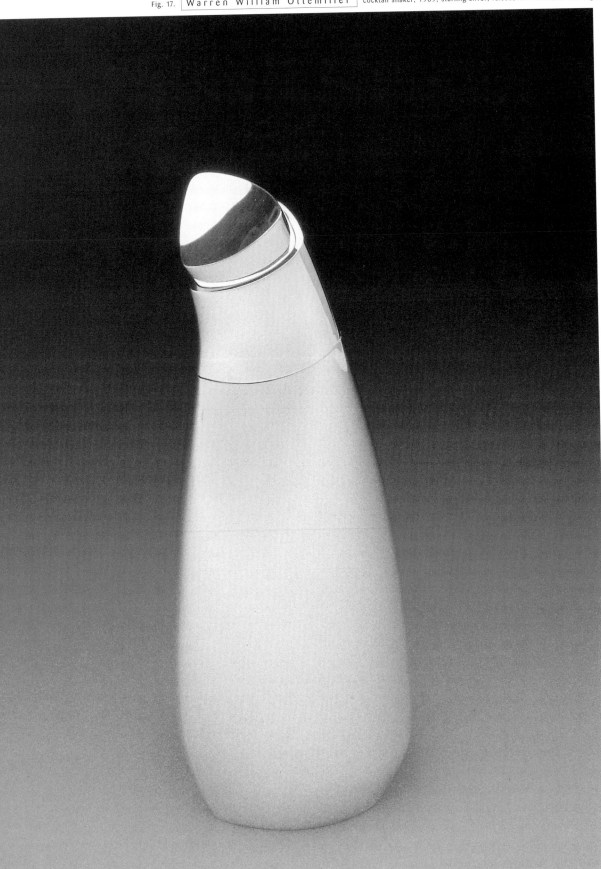

The 1960s:

A Surge in Crafts

Schools

In Canada, as in other countries, the 1960s were marked by demonstrations and protests. Students marched, hippies promoted flower power, women experienced a raising of consciousness, and the disillusioned formed back-to-the-land communes. An understandable backlash against postwar consumerism and materialism promoted new lifestyles, which often involved rock music, drugs and natural fibres. Woodstock, one of the most famous international gatherings of the period, was advertised at the time as the *Woodstock Music and Art Fair*. The world of craft was valued for its integrity, simplicity and emphasis on handwork.

While schools such as Mount Allison University and OCA offered good metal programs in the 1940s and early 1950s, they were hardly typical of metalsmithing programs, which tended to be trade oriented, recreational, or aimed at occupational therapy. In such courses, designs were often stereotyped or even taken from patterns. Canada's first industrial-design program began at OCA in 1947. The college aimed to give industrial-design students a thorough knowledge of materials and production techniques. Silversmithing skills were particularly useful for the industrial designer, who needed to be able to produce prototypes for industry. Like design programs in other countries, many graduates went on to become teachers or studio craftspeople, rather than going into industry.

During the postwar era, few Canadian students were able to be trained for the gold and silversmithing profession in a dedicated, intensive European-style program. The Ontario Craft Foundation, founded in 1966 to fill the void in craft education, was concerned that Ontario "was not creating its own unique designs in craft and industry." It judged Canada as "too much a nation of copiers of the design of others." The Foundation recommended the establishment of a school of craft and design that would train craftspeople who would work in their own studios, teach, or go into industry. Nineteen sixty-seven saw the opening of the Sheridan College School of Design, in Mississauga. This school was unique in Canada, and according to its aims, was determined "not only to embody the best of European and American design schools but to create its own Canadian character."

With the School of Design came a new metal program. Haakon Bakken, a jeweller who trained in Oslo, Norway, and at the School for American Craftsmen, in Rochester, New York, took charge of the program. Philip Morton, who had established the contemporary jewellery and three-dimensional design program at the University of Minnesota, joined the staff for the 1968–69 year. Subsequently, Warren William (Bill) Ottemiller (for an example of his work, see Fig. 17), also an MFA graduate of the School for American Craftsmen, joined the faculty.

Because of its proximity to Southern Ontario, the School for American Craftsmen had a significant effect on Ontario metalsmithing. The school's early influence, with instructors John Prip and Hans Christiansen, was strongly Danish Modern. Many Ontarians took degrees at the school, and metalsmiths from the school, including Albert Paley, frequently acted as lecturers and jurors in Toronto.

According to Sheridan's director, Donald McKinley, most Sheridan students went into crafts because they wanted "direct involvement with the material." A foundation year required them to study design and art history and to work in wood, metal, ceramics and fibre. The sense of excitement at Sheridan was further fuelled by interaction between the various craft studios. A student raising a teapot in metal could discuss shape and pouring function with a potter who threw far more teapots than the metalsmith.

With a maximum enrollment of two hundred, Sheridan's purpose was to prepare students for careers in craft or design. Of Sheridan students, the Ontario Craft Foundation offered this optimistic proclamation: "They shall become the experts — the professionals." Their aspirations were soon rewarded, and the work of Sheridan students and graduates began to become noticed in juried metal exhibitions. The work was well designed, and its artistic approach was experimental and fresh. Distinctions between art and craft were to blur. Some graduates went into jewellery manufacturing, but it was usually a short period of time before they returned to the studio environment.

In Halifax, NSCAD revivified its jewellery department with the appointment of Orland Larson in 1968. Larson laid the foundation for the program within an art college, which became noted for espousing a conceptual approach to art. In 1969, the college took out an advertisement in *Time* magazine, asking, in bold letters, "What is art?" The reply of the college was that it did not know what art was but believed that was the way it should be. The college did, however, have firm ideas about what design should be, and it intended to be the best in North America for both art and design.

Larson was enthusiastic about art education and craft development in Canada. He held a degree in art education from the University of Wisconsin, had studied with metalsmith Stanley Lechtzin at the Tyler School of Art in Philadelphia, and had done doctoral work at Columbia University, in New York City. Larson was able to convince the administration at NSCAD of the need for a jewellery department as part of the craft division. Within ten years, the school established a two-year masters of fine arts program in jewellery and metalsmithing, with Zoe Lucas as the first graduate.

The strength of NSCAD's craft division, which included instruction in ceramics, metal and fibre, allowed it to continue under the fine arts rubric, while most college fine arts departments concentrated on painting and sculpture. According to Larson, the jewellery program "emphasized the aesthetic side of jewellery making" and students were attracted to it because they not only learned the fundamentals of working with metal, but also "how to resolve problems in a creative way."

Norwegian goldsmith Christian Gaudernack would later spend a total of seven years at NSCAD (throughout the seventies and early eighties) and would leave the strong imprint of his minimal forms and perfect craftsmanship. He emphasized abstract and formal concerns and, along with Larson, was important in building bridges between NSCAD and European jewellers. The program was further enriched with a large number of visiting national and international artists, including the influential German sculptor and jeweller Klaus Bury.

The college's energetic approach carried into the jewellery studio, where there was a stringent querying of intent. Students were challenged to explain their concept for any given piece, and to defend their choice of material and technique. A demand for visual and historical research and written work resulted in jewellers who were articulate about their craft.

George Brown College, formerly the Provincial Institute of Trades, had a somewhat different approach from Sheridan and NSCAD. The program at George Brown was closely allied with the jewellery trade and aimed to provide technicians for industry. George Brown graduates were usually better trained in technique than in design. But art-college graduates sometimes went to George Brown for additional technical education, and conversely, George Brown graduates sometimes went on to art colleges for further design training. This trade-versus-art dichotomy was common in other parts of the world as well. Schools in England and Germany were known for their emphasis on either trade or art. The best designers often resisted working for commercial enterprises, and the trade's most skilled makers were often uncomfortable with the ways of college art departments. It was only after the Second World War that the Royal College of Art, in London, began to draw upon trade jewellers and metalsmiths as teachers, in a renewed mandate to improve British manufacturing.

The Institute of Technology and Art, in Alberta, moved its courses to the Alberta College of Art in the late 1960s. Frank X. Phillips, a well-known engraver who had studied at the School for American Craftsmen, planned a full-time jewellery program for the College of Art. Bev de Jong and Harold O'Connor taught in the department in the early 1970s and helped to establish this important program in the prairie provinces. Orland Larson took over in 1979 and remained for eleven years.

In Quebec, under the government of Jean Lesage, major changes were made in education that would benefit arts and crafts. The CEGEPs were begun in 1967 and would later incorporate jewellery programs. The Saidye Bronfman Centre opened in Montreal in 1967, offering jewellery classes in addition to the general-arts training provided by the Écoles des Beaux-Arts in Quebec City and Montreal. After 1962, the École de Claude Bérubé, in Montreal, offered courses in enamelling.

In the 1960s, jewellery and metal arts became part of professional craft training and broadened provincial educational programs. Perhaps most important to the development of metal artists was the inclusion of metal arts in college-level programs. This further opened the door for personal and artistic expression in jewellery and hollowware.

Other Educational Approaches

In addition to the college programs, metal associations in Nova Scotia, Ontario and British Columbia continued to play an important role in the education of craftspeople. MAG Ontario voted to continue its membership in the American Craftsmen's Educational Council, especially as it received a forty percent discount on slides and films. Meetings would often include a film from Handy and Harman on some aspect of metalsmithing.

Fig. 18. Tommia Vaughan-Jones (left) and unidentified woman at exhibition opening, Royal Ontario Museum, 1962. Photo: *Toronto Star*

Other popular techniques that were demonstrated included the fusing of metals without solder and the reticulating of the surface of metals. Arthur Korber, a German-trained jeweller, demonstrated a technique for making niello, and Sylvia Hahn showed a method of gilding on sterling spoons with linen ash.

While MAG Ontario also had a social function, which was especially evident at exhibition openings (see Fig. 18), there was always a strong emphasis on design education. Lectures were held on designing rings and flatware, and meetings provided opportunities for members to have their work professionally critiqued. Harold Stacey referred to some of the members as "rabidly" professional, and hoped that all would keep the "dedicated attitude of the lover or amateur of great craft traditions."

MAG Ontario discouraged "hobbicraft," which it interpreted as poor-quality work turned out as cheap souvenirs or as gifts for the maker's friends. Although a good percentage of its members were amateurs, the guild always encouraged members to create good-quality metalwork. The annual show was always juried — usually by a combination of professional members and outside jurors from museums or art schools — which helped to maintain the standard of work shown publicly. The Steel Trophy, for best-in-show, was made by Harold Stacey in 1957 in honour of George Steel, a well-known lapidarist. It was awarded annually (with one exception) until the exhibition became biannual in 1994.

In British Columbia, the Creative Jewellers Guild enacted a bylaw requiring new members to design and make a piece of jewellery incorporating in some manner the lines of the Guild's logo. Since 1961, the guild has selected an annual theme, and members are expected to create a piece using the year's theme as inspiration. Because of the proximity to Washington and Oregon, the guild soon became associated with jewellery groups across the border, and they began to share workshops and exhibitions.

The Department of Industry and Development of the Province of New Brunswick, following the Second World War, provided education in craft to encourage the development of cottage industries. In 1954, Barth and Lucie Wttewaall, immigrants from the Netherlands, signed up for a two-week jewellery-making course, which was held in their own home in Sussex, New Brunswick. Seven months later, at the CNE, they took first place for a silver necklace with black stones. They con-

tinued to win prizes at the CNE through the 1960s. The couple took unusually shaped stones and set them in sterling silver, using their horticultural background as inspiration for their flower and leaf forms. Lucie Wttewaall, who had attended art school in Amsterdam, taught jewellery at the Craft School in Fredericton from 1957 to 1979, and received recognition from the Canadian Crafts Council in 1980 for her outstanding contributions to the field. Along with potters Kjeld and Erica Deichmann, the Wttewaal's are considered founders of the modern craft movement in New Brunswick.

The Canadian Jewellers Association has been another educational force in Canada. Its members — mostly commercial and manufacturing jewellers — have contributed to awards and encouraged gemmology courses in jewellery programs. Its publication, *Canadian Jeweller,* has featured articles on art jewellers, and for a period its trade fairs highlighted the work of graduating students from college programs across the country.

Refiners of precious metals also had an educational role. Many opened their refining and casting operations for public tours and demonstrations. The advent of better centrifugal and vacuum casting machines after the Second World War made casting work easier for the jeweller. As with most technical advances, a period of experimentation ensued. To distinguish their work from commercial jewellery cast with the aid of rubber molds, art jewellers, after an initial period of involvement, employed personalized casting methods or moved to other techniques.

Apprenticeship was another means of learning jewellery skills. In 1969, Michael and Paula Letki arrived in Toronto from Loughborough College of Art and Design, in England. Soon they set up Letki Designs, a studio and sales area on Baldwin Street in midtown Toronto. Many of their several dozen apprentices would go on to become well-established Canadian jewellers, including Martha Glenny and Oksana Kit. The Letki's formula for success involved good design (for an example of their work, see Plate 5), a limited production line, and effective communication with a clientele quite new to commissioned work. Their ability to "work as one person" enabled their pioneering retail studio to thrive until 1991.

Apprenticing abroad was an adventuresome route to learning jewellery technique and design. Jacques Troalen, after his training with Montreal jeweller Georges Schwartz, received a Canada Council

Grant in 1969 to study in Europe. For a year and a half he worked under various masters: Ernest Blyth and Frances Beck, in London; Sigurd Persson and Olle Olhsson, in Stockholm; and Wulf Bélard in Brugg, Switzerland. Troalen readily admitted that the Scandinavian influences were the strongest. His subsequent work, including an 18-karat-gold necklace entitled *Psyche* (Fig. 19), was pure and clean in design. Troalen learned well the Scandinavian lessons of clarity of shape and nobility of material.

The establishment of the Society of North American Goldsmiths (SNAG) was an answer to the need for a forum in which artists, craftspeople and educators could share the information, ideas and problems they encountered. SNAG was the brainchild of Philip Morton, who suggested the need for such a conference to colleagues in both Canada and the U.S. during his time at Sheridan College. Of the eighteen founding members that met in 1969, three were Canadian — Hero Kielman, Harold Stacey, and Orland Larson. According to Kurt Matzdorf, in *The Founding Masters,* they proposed to raise "standards in both design and craftsmanship over those then prevailing in the field." The organization grew to become the most important force in the development of art jewellery and metal in North America. Its conferences, exhibitions and workshops — and especially its publication, *Metalsmith* — provided the dynamism and artistic validation sought by its American and Canadian founders.

Public Awareness

Educating craftspeople was only half of the equation in improving the lot of Canadian jewellery. The other half was helping the public to understand and appreciate handmade contemporary jewellery and hollowware. The guilds in Nova Scotia, Ontario and British Columbia enlisted craftspeople for public demonstrations of metal forming and raising. They also ran booths at craft and civic events. The members of MAG Ontario arranged for a MAG show to tour to other Canadian cities. Tommia Vaughan-Jones, among others, gave lectures and guided gallery tours, pointing out features of handmade jewellery and hollowware to a public that often did not know the difference between sterling and plated silver.

Every practicing jeweller also played a part in educating the public. When Montreal jeweller Georges Schwartz came to Canada in the 1950s, he realized that there was no real appreciation for coloured stones in fine jewellery. Gold and diamonds were the order of the day, and rings were most in demand. His magnificent training at the exclusive Parisian jewellery firm of Van Cleef and Arpels was underused. He had to create a clientele. In doing so he found that French Canadians were "more open, but less fortunate," so for them he designed pieces with more style and less material content (for an example of his work, see Fig. 20).

Schwartz would eventually be rewarded for his time spent introducing new ideas to the Canadian market. By the 1970s, Schwartz felt that a "Montreal School of Jewellery" had developed, with a style of its own. Characterized by bold pieces with smooth, coloured stones, it was a style halfway between the complex richness of French jewellery and the more quiet simplicity of North American jewellery.

The Quebec public also endorsed the work of the enamelling team of Yves Sylvestre and Micheline de Passillé. Their pieces, inspired by nature, were popular not only for their intrinsic beauty, but also as expressions of Quebec culture. Demand was so great that de Passillé and Sylvestre established a production-type business that employed others in various stages of the enamelling process. More Quebec enamellists followed suit until the market slackened in the 1980s.

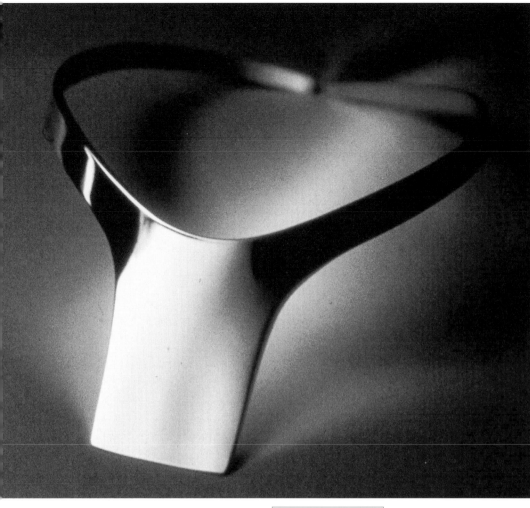

Fig. 19. | J a c q u e s   T r o a l e n | Psyche, 1974, neckpiece, 18-karat gold.

Fig. 20. | G e o r g e s   S c h w a r t z | Qui suis-je?, 1985, brooch, 18-karat yellow gold, black opal, 70 x 45 mm.

Pat Hunt brooch, 1971, sterling silver, reticulated, fabricated, 7.5 x 2.5 cm.

For some emerging art jewellers, craft shows became a popular way to earn money and reach new audiences. The sixties hippie lifestyle suited the individualism of many young jewellers, who set up showcases or black-velvet-covered tables to sell their wares. Craft shows were used as stepping stones to more permanent selling arrangements with galleries and shops. In Quebec, the first *Salon des métiers d'art du Québec* was held in the Montreal subway. It has continued as an important venue for some Quebec artists.

Liturgical Metalwork

Churches and synagogues have been among the foremost patrons of gold and silversmiths for centuries. Quebec churches especially boast a rich body of liturgical silver. Immediately following the Second World War, commissions of religious objects were an important part of Canadian metalsmithing. Religious work in metal has traditionally been prescribed by liturgical conventions and commissioned by church or synagogue committees. As a result it has often lacked in excitement. But two exhibitions in the 1960s grappled with what the Very Reverend William Bothwell of Christ Church Deanery, in Montreal, called contemporary art's search for "meaning in a world which is full of revolt and cruelty." The exhibitions, entitled *Canadian Religious Art Today,* were presented by Regis College, the Jesuit Seminary in Toronto. They encompassed work by over a hundred visual artists and sculptors as well as several metal artists. In the 1966 exhibition, Ludwig Nickel showed a red enamel chalice and Harold Stacey showed

a sterling silver communion flagon. Helga Palko entered a bishop's ring and an ivory carving with a silver mount. Jack Sullivan, an instructor at OCA, showed welded steel and bronze pieces. Marc André Beaudin, professor of enamelwork and jewellery in the Faculty of Arts at the University of Sherbrooke, showed two raised chalices. The abstract modern aesthetic of the L'Art Sacré movement, which had begun in France but influenced many Quebec artists, was evident in the exhibition. Although commission work continued, it was at a much-reduced pace after the liturgical changes of Vatican II. There has not been a national show of religious art since the sixties.

One of the most prolific silversmiths specializing in liturgical metal has been Gilles Beaugrand, of Montreal, who studied at the École des beaux-arts in Montreal and in France. Beaugrand began designing chalices in 1932, at a time when much of Quebec's religious silver was still imported from Europe. With over sixty years of designing and making, more than eleven thousand chalices — for priests, bishops and two popes — bear the signature of Beaugrand. In collaboration with the firm Desmarais & Robitaille, Beaugrand's work continues to be sold across North America.

Women and Jewellery

In the forties and early fifties, men outnumbered women in silver-smithing by about two to one, and there were few women teaching metal at the college level. Lois E. Betteridge, a member of the first graduating class in metal at the University of Kansas, in 1952, opened her studio in Toronto that same year and began teaching design at Ryerson Polytechnical Institute. Vera McIntyre Cryderman created a vocational art department at H.B. Beal Technical School in London, Ontario, and was well known for her jewellery. Norah Goreham, of Halifax, taught jewellery through a provincial government program in Nova Scotia in the sixties and seventies. Christel-Elvira Klocke arrived as a master jeweller at George Brown College in 1968.

Ontario boasted many fine female jewellers during the sixties, including Tommia Vaughan-Jones, Joyce Merrifield, Joyce Turnbull, Mary Milne, Pat Hunt, Reeva Perkins and Helga Palko. Although all were not professional, the refinement and imagination of their work led the jury for the 1965 Canadian Guild of Crafts (Ontario) Show to remark that the jewellery showed real "flair and elegance."

Pat Hunt and Reeva Perkins, sisters who had trained together at the Provincial Institute of Trades in Toronto, showed particularly elegant work. Their sterling silver pieces depicted strong organic forms with no obvious influences. Hunt's brooch (Fig. 21) had a reticulated surface, a popular sixties technique, but its elongated form stretched beyond the usual size of a brooch.

Perkins carried off the Steel Trophy at MAG Ontario's 1968 show with a neckpiece of alternating positive and negative cutouts (Fig. 22). In 1975, the International Year of Women, Perkins would be commissioned by the Ontario Provincial Government to design a pin to honour twenty-six outstanding women. She created an appealing trillium pin (Fig. 23), the petals of which, constructed in sterling silver, were gently shaped and softly finished, with a native amethyst as the focal point. It represented both the directness of the best jewellery of the time and the rising status of women in society.

Fig. 22. <u>Reeva Perkins</u> neckpiece, 1968, sterling silver, fabricated, 41 cm. long. Photo: Jeremy Jones.

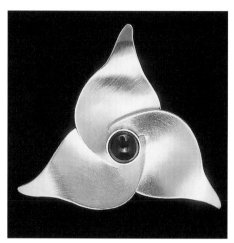

Fig. 23. | Reeva Perkins | brooch, 1975, sterling silver, amethyst, fabricated, 6 x 6 x 1 cm. Photo: Jeremy Jones.

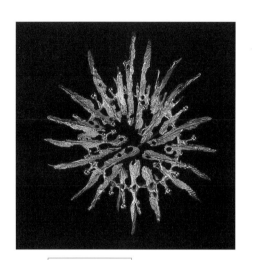

Fig. 24. | Helga Palko | brooch, 1966, gold, cast.

Helga Palko, who graduated from the Vienna Academy of Fine Arts and studied at the California College of Arts and Crafts in Oakland, gave week-long workshops in jewellery and enamels sponsored by the Saskatchewan Arts Board. She was especially known for her large-scale enamel projects, such as those completed for the outside of a church in Lumsden, Saskatchewan, in 1958. Her approach to jewellery during the sixties is exemplified by a striking gold brooch (Fig. 24), which featured striated elements that radiated in a centripetal pattern like a starburst. Cast by the lost-wax method, this piece marked a change from forged and fabricated work and pointed the way for the cast jewellery of the 1970s. It was shown in *Canadian Fine Crafts/Artisanat Canadien 1966/67,* an exhibition held at the National Gallery. Palko was later head of the Fine Metals Department at Algonquin College, from 1971 to 1982.

Exhibitions

Canada celebrated its one hundredth birthday at *Expo '67* in Montreal. Considering the lack of a fine jewellery tradition in Canada, the sheer number of Canadian jewellers at *Expo '67* was remarkable. Thirty jewellers from across the country were represented in the Canadian Pavilion in a show called *Canadian Fine Crafts*, which was intended as a "cross-reference survey of craftsmanship in Canada."

Moncrieff Williamson, who put the collection together, was "particularly impressed with the rich variety in craftsmanship practiced by the jewellers" and "the superb quality of French Canadian enamellists." The show featured chalices and enamels by Gilles Beaugrand, Monique Drolet-Coté, and Bernard Chaudron. There were also important pieces of fine jewellery by jewellers who had immigrated to Canada after the war — Cavelti, Schluep, Gehrig, Kielman and Palko. The high regard placed on the gold and silversmiths of the period was a reflection of the quality work of these masters.

In 1969, *Craft Dimensions Canada,* a national exhibition, was jointly staged by the Canadian Guild of Crafts (Ontario) and the Royal Ontario Museum. One juror, American silversmith Ronald Pearson, chose as his favourite piece a silver pin with iron pyrite crystals, made by Bev de Jong, of Alberta. Other award winners were Lois Etherington Betteridge, for a pitcher and a ring, and Orland Larson for a silver-and-bronze comb.

The world's first international exhibition of modern jewellery was held in 1961 at the Goldsmiths' Hall in London. Such an extensive show was unprecedented — there were over a thousand pieces of jewellery from twenty-eight countries. Canadians Toni Cavelti, Georges Delrue, Pius Kaufman and Thomas Primavesi were among those selected for the exhibition. Their work was later documented in Graham Hughes's book, *Modern Jewelry,* the first comprehensive survey of jewellery in the twentieth century.

In general, Canadian metalwork of the 1960s was approached from a design perspective and still showed a Scandinavian influence. Fine jewellers such as Cavelti and Schluep usually worked in gold, but the favoured metal of rank-and-file metalsmiths was sterling silver. As ornament, neckpieces and pendants were becoming larger and more imposing. Techniques such as reticulation and fusing offered variety in surface texture, as did various casting media. Abstract designs made from flowing and textured wax were another sign of the period.

Brooches and rings were popular and showed a freedom of form seldom seen before; large, free-form cut stones were thought to be more interesting than formally cut stones. The leaf and flower motifs of the forties and fifties had been replaced with abstract organic shapes that reflected the sixties zeitgeist.

Pop art, with its ironic jabs at consumerism, did not have as much influence in Canada during the sixties as it did in the United States. Because its approach was somewhat anti-design, it would take until the eighties before it would show up in Canadian pieces such as David Swinson's *Tuna/Thon* (Plate 6). The educational advances of the sixties set the stage for the generation that would follow the postwar European masters. New attitudes toward individualism wrought by the sixties would lead to the conceptual breakthroughs and materials experimentation of the seventies and eighties.

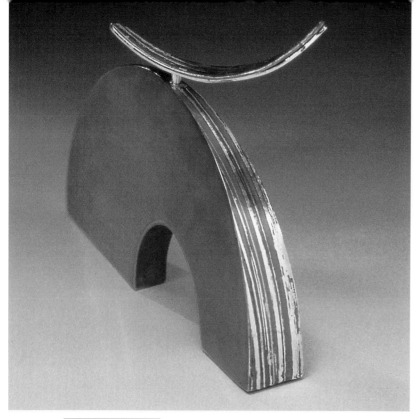

Fig. 25. | Aggie Beynon | perfume bottle, 1983, powdered metal (pure silver and pure copper), copper, sterling silver, fabricated, 15 x 20 x 5 cm.

Fig. 26. | Sandra Noble Goss | neckpiece (detail), 1977, sterling silver, acrylic, fabricated, 30 cm. long.

44

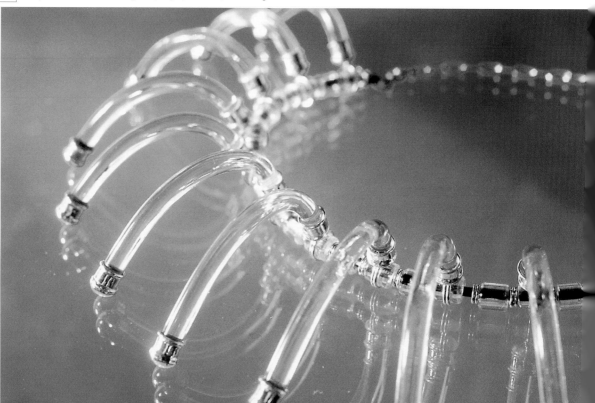

The 1970s:

Material Explorations

New and Alternative Materials

Industrial designer Sid Bersudsky caused a heated discussion at a meeting of MAG Ontario one evening in 1967, when he accused craftspeople of not making the best use of the materials and methods at hand. He further accused craftspeople of being snobbish, and uninterested in technological advances. Bersudsky added that by using ancient methods, craftspeople were not fully accomplishing the most they could.

The choice between slower, more traditional and costly methods and new technologies has presented a consistent dilemma for metalsmiths. Regardless, with new metals and new techniques, the seventies saw an expansion of the smith's repertoire. Among the materials that became popular in the seventies were refractory (or reactive) metals, which had not previously been available commercially. The research department of the Worshipful Company of Goldsmiths, in London, had much to do with the introduction of these metals, and jewellers were intrigued with the phenomenal color possibilities they offered. Titanium, niobium and tantalum have become the most popular refractory metals for jewellery making. These metals, which are extremely hard, do not rust, but form a surface oxide film when charged with low voltages of electricity. Through careful control of the voltage, almost any colour can be achieved. Historically, gemstones and enamels had offered colour in jewellery. But with the advent of these refractory metals, the medium itself allowed for strong colour without the weight or fragility of enamel or the expense of stones.

Pamela Ritchie, in Halifax, created a thoughtful series of brooches entitled *The Twelve Children of Niobe* (for an example, see Plate 7) that pointed to the classical origins of the names of the new refractory metals. Niobe (niobium) was a woman in Greek mythology who was turned to stone by Zeus for boasting about her children. Tantalus (tantalum) and Titan (titanium) belonged to a mythological race of earth giants. Each brooch was subtly coloured, and while stones and silver were incorporated, the niobium remained the central focus. Ritchie pleated the niobium using a sewing technique that perfectly suited the lightweight metal and reinforced the maternal connotations of the title.

The first Canadians to explore titanium fully were the Toronto jewellery team of David McAleese and Alison Wiggins. With a background in lapidary, they conducted research to find the most effective techniques for cutting and colouring the metal. Their reward was apparent in their creation of a series of lively pen-shaped pins with fuschia and blue bands (Plate 8). They created another series of soft geometric pins that displayed up to twenty hues each. Their successful experimentation with colour found a public eager for this space-age metal.

The anodization of aluminum, a relatively inexpensive soft metal, opened another door to colour. In anodization, aluminum is electrochemically treated to create a colour surface film that is sealed to prevent corrosion. As with titanium, many artists were attracted by the colour possibilities of this lightweight material.

In the late seventies, Neil Carrick Aird, a graduate of the Glasgow School of Art, in Scotland, and owner of Metalworks Contemporary Goldsmithing, in Kingston, Ontario, became involved in research into the properties of aluminum and niobium. With the help of the research department of the Aluminum Company of Canada, Aird, while teaching master at St. Lawrence College, experimented with the fusing of layers of aluminum and niobium. He would then cut through the layers and colour them. The effect was an intense landscape of metals with naturally merging colours, which Aird fenced with gold to form a brooch (see Plate 9). According to Aird, it was an expression in metal of his abiding penchant both for landscape and small things.

Fig. 27. **Kim Dickinson** brooch, 1979, acrylic, sterling silver, 6 x 7 x 1.2 cm.

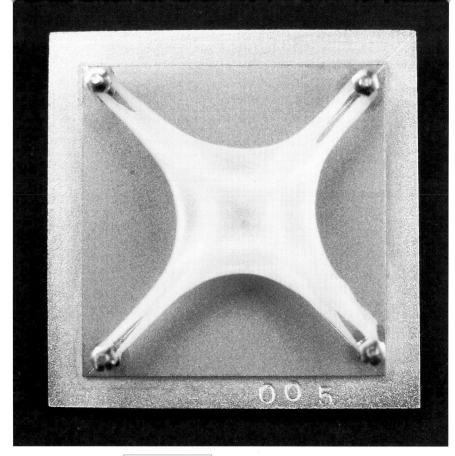

Fig. 28. │ J a m e s   E v a n s │ one of a series of nine brooches, 1981, latex, sterling silver, steel, brass, fabricated, 5 x 5 cm.

47

Another aspect of metal was explored by Aggie Beynon, of Waterloo, Ontario, during this period. In a metallurgy class at the University of Kansas, Beynon began looking into the properties of powdered metal. Her research led her to produce fusions of powdered copper, gold and silver. These were heated in a non-oxidizing atmosphere and rolled into sheets that produced unusually coloured and textured surfaces. Her perfume bottle (Fig. 25) is a fine example of how she incorporated this technique into her work.

Plastics had been used for jewellery for decades, but in the late sixties and the seventies they became popular alternatives for other materials such as ivory and bone, as well as being appreciated for their own properties. While teaching at Sheridan College's metal studio, Greg Merrall designed a series of rings constructed entirely of laminated coloured acrylics. At *Goldsmith '70,* the inaugural show of SNAG, held at the Minnesota Museum of Art, Wendy Shingler exhibited a ring made with laminated acrylic and set in a sterling silver box. Viewed from above, the ring was pink-and-blue striped, but from the side it appeared purple.

One of the most dynamic acrylic pieces made in Canada in the seventies was a necklace by Sandra Noble Goss, of Owen Sound, Ontario. Goss cut clear acrylic rods, which she then bent and capped with silver tubing (Fig. 26). The even spacing of the elements made the neckpiece seem classical, yet the use of plastic lent it a contemporary air.

In 1979, Kim Dickinson, of Toronto, won best-in-show at MAG Ontario's *The Medium is Metal* show, with a brooch made mostly of acrylic (Fig. 27). The brooch — in contrasting bone and clear sandblasted acrylic, with cast silver to hold the parts together — featured finely sculpted organic elements. The interesting paradox was that, while the guild and its shows promoted the use of metal, some of the most adventuresome designs contained more plastics than metal. The combination of acrylics and metals continued into the eighties with pieces such as James Evans's latex and sterling silver brooch (Fig. 28). To the guild's credit, it did not discourage such submissions of alternative materials, but merely requested that pieces submitted contain *some* metal.

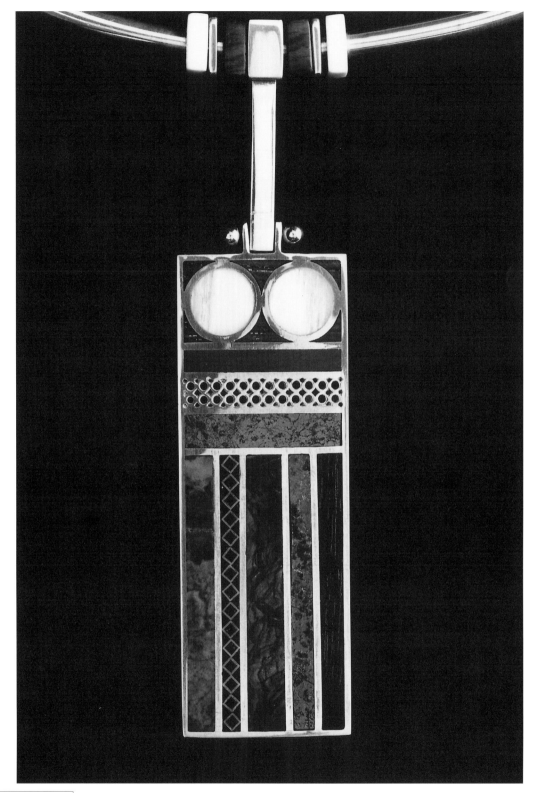

48

Fig. 29. | Donald Stuart | neckpiece, 1976, sterling silver, rosewood, pyrite, jasper, onyx, bournite, ebony, narwhal ivory, fabricated, inlaid, 18.5 x 22.5 cm.

Don Stuart, Head of the Jewellery and Metals program at Georgian College, in Barrie, Ontario, used materials such as whalebone, caribou antler and walrus tusk in his jewellery. Stuart employed time-honoured cloisonné techniques to arrange these materials in abstract patterns. His award-winning 1976 neckpiece (Fig. 29) confirmed his keen sense of pattern and texture. Stuart spent time teaching weaving in the Arctic, but his modern use of bone and stone is more inspired by Inuit culture than appropriated from it. "My work is contemporary in approach," Stuart explains, "but rooted in tradition." Stuart would continue to explore the inlay technique into the eighties and nineties. In 1986, Stuart was commissioned to create a piece for Canadian composer R. Murray Schafer, the first recipient of the Glenn Gould prize. He designed a sterling silver rose bowl, with a central medallion inlaid with naturally occurring Canadian materials, such as sodalite, silver ore, agate, gold, walnut, and labradorite, and augmented with sapphires — Gould's birthstone (Fig. 30).

49

Fig. 30. Donald Stuart presentation rendering for rose bowl commissioned to accompany the Glenn Gould Prize awarded to Canadian composer R. Murray Schafer, 1987, sterling silver, 18-karat gold, sodalite, silver ore, agate, walnut burl, labradorite, sapphires, 28 x 11 cm.

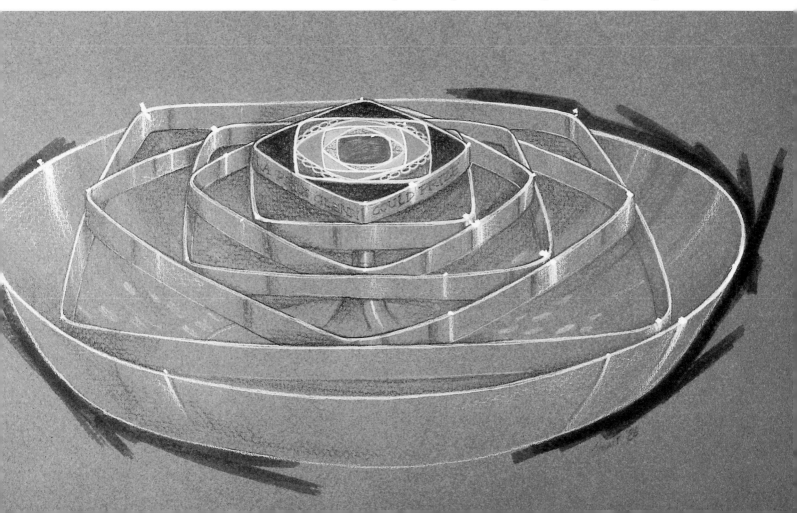

Other jewellers also looked to nature for materials to mix with their metal. Colleen McCallum, of Toronto, chose rabbit fur to line her silver boxes (Fig. 31), and Sherry Otterway used the skull of a turtle for her neckpiece *When All Else Fails* (Fig. 45). Such combinations of materials were sometimes chosen for their shock value, but just as often they represented the artist's view that all materials — natural and refined — were valuable for their unique physical properties. Bones, fur and feathers were among the earliest forms of adornment. The use of Canadian species has also been a way of expressing Canadian identity.

Techniques

Concurrent with experimentation in new and alternative materials was a renewed interest in historical techniques. It was generally felt that the greater the number of technical options for interpreting a design idea, the more successful the realization would be. A number of Americans came to Canada during the seventies to demonstrate their research. Jeweller John Paul Miller conducted a workshop for MAG Ontario on granulation, an ancient and mysterious technique, perfected by the Etruscans, in which fine metal beads are fused to a metal surface. Arline Fisch, author of *Textile Techniques in Metal,* conducted a workshop at Sheridan College on weaving and knitting with metal.

Other techniques that resurfaced included inlaying of coloured metals, acid etching and electroforming (a process in which metal is electrodeposited onto a matrix). Chasing and repoussé, which had never left the metal repertoire, was coupled with contemporary designs for a new effect. Vanessa Compton, a graduate of Sheridan College, determined that wax casting was her medium and created a kingdom of mythical animals that included *Dragon Going Under the Wave of Life* (Fig. 32). Compton's success showed that even in a period where the strongest influences were for clean surfaces and abstraction, diversity was welcome.

The seemingly mundane technique of polishing underwent greater scrutiny during the seventies, and jurors often found fault with finishes. Some less-experienced craftsmen experimented with form but found that they were unable to successfully polish their pieces due to fire scale, a dark oxide coating that forms when metal is heated. Students were also full of ideas but often lacked the time and critical awareness to finish a piece well for a deadline. The unforgiving nature of metal meant that a simple miscalculation might not appear until the final polishing. Despite all of this, there was a gradual evolution in finishing approaches after the sixties. A highly polished piece was once the mark of an expert silversmith; however, a new appreciation developed for lower lustre brushed and stoned finishes. These provided greater contrasts when used with gold and other precious metals, and were easier to maintain. They also looked more contemporary.

While the accumulation of technical skills was laudable, there were instances when it did not result in better jewellery. As Bev de Jong commented to *Arts West* in 1975: "Technical skill is a discipline which must be laboured at, until slowly it melts away completely and just happens as the idea develops… It is easy to overpower the idea by a powerful display of decoration or fancy technique."

50

51

Fig. 32. │ V a n e s s a C o m p t o n │ Dragon Going Under the Wave of Life (ring), 1976, sterling silver. Photo: Peter Hogan.

Exhibitions

In 1971, the Women's Committee of the Art Gallery of Ontario staged a most impressive international exhibition and sale entitled *Jewelry 71*. Work by professional metalsmiths stood alongside jewellery made or designed by painters and sculptors. In all there were more than a hundred pieces, including work by Pablo Picasso, the Pomodoro brothers of Italy, Irena Brynner, Alexander Calder, Klaus Bury, Albert Paley, José de Rivera, Oleg Skoogfors and Heiki Seppa, and by Canadians Haaken Bakken, Lois E. Betteridge, Ronald Bloore, Georges Delrue, Pat Hunt, Christel E. Klocke, Orland Larson, Ludwig Nickel, Dora de Pedery-Hunt, Alan and Reeva Perkins, Bill Reid, Walter Schluep, Victor Secrett and Willy van Yperen.

The high-profile affair provided a fine arts boost to the jewellery community, while calling attention to the uneasy relationship between art jewellery and public art galleries. Picasso, Calder and Lichtenstein could have any of their work, whether jewellery or paintings, hung on the gallery's walls. In contrast, the work of jewellers was rarely exhibited or collected by art galleries, or even by museums. Instead, it was sold in gallery retail shops such as the one at the Art Gallery of Ontario, where Carol Rapp and her successors promoted and sold the work of hundreds of Canadian art jewellers. Those who enjoyed contemporary art often bought jewellery that shared the same inspiration and ideas. The irony was that profits from jewellery sales were used to help purchase paintings and sculptures for the gallery's permanent collections. The art-craft dichotomy meant that there was no mandate for the gallery to collect contemporary jewellery.

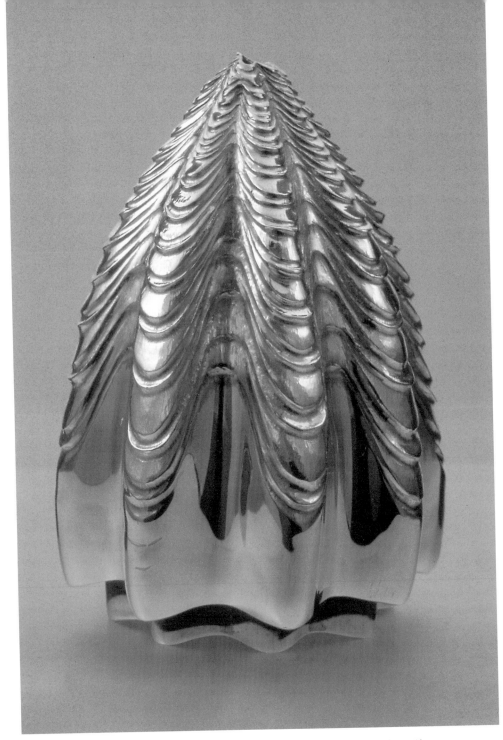

52

Fig. 34. Lois E. Betteridge Spice Shaker, 1977, sterling silver, raised, chased and repousséd, 10 cm. high. Photo: Keith Betteridge.

With the intriguing title, *Make (māk)*, the Canadian Guild of Crafts (Ontario) and the Ontario Science Centre collaborated to hold an exhibition of contemporary crafts in 1971. The show was juried by the well-known Canadian architect and craft supporter Raymond Moriyama, who explained that he made his selection of works based on the "potential to enhance and to intensify the joy of the everyday." Moriyama concluded that Canadian crafts had the potential to reach the level of international stature. Of the work selected, Christel Elvira Klocke's brooch of gold and tourmaline-quartz crystal (Fig. 33) was deemed the "best piece of jewellery." Its natural setting of rough-cut stone in a field of textured gold segments made a perfectly unified and imaginative presentation. While it did not apply to Klocke's piece, Ian Bolton, of Birks and Sons, was disturbed that a surprising number of submissions had no final finishing. He complained: "some pieces even have a fire skin still on them with no attempt at polishing."

Artisan '78 was the first national travelling exhibition of Canadian crafts ever to cross the country. Organized by the Canadian Crafts Council, it was supported by Jean A. Chalmers, Wintario and the Museum Assistance Program of the National Museums of Canada. Works by one hundred and twenty-two craftspeople — from all ten provinces and the Northwest Territories — were represented. Ultimately, all of the pieces were given to the Museum of Civilization to comprise the Jean A. Chalmers National Craft Collection. The Chalmers Collection represented metalsmiths in a wide variety of styles and approaches. For example, Jeffrey Gabriel, of Oka, Quebec, showed a silver beaker with inlaid stone. Gabriel was a student of Gilles Beaugrand, and his work reflected a French design influence. Earl Muldoe expressed Native tradition in his engraved silver *Ksan Box*, and Theo Janson used stars, bubbles and other figures in a whimsical belt buckle. The success of the exhibition was a testimony to the varied and healthy state of the craft.

The Saidye Bronfman Award for Craft

In 1978, Lois Etherington Betteridge, educated at OCA, the University of Kansas and Cranbrook Academy, received the Saidye Bronfman Award, the highest recognition for excellence in craftsmanship in Canada. The award was established by the Bronfman Family Foundation in 1977 to acknowledge not only technical mastery, but also innovation, creativity and aesthetics. According to the jury, Betteridge was a "sensitive artist ... in harmony with her medium." In a post-industrial age, Betteridge still spends an average of twelve hours a day in raising complex forms from flat sheets of silver. She then embellishes the forms with chasing and repoussé. Betteridge's spice shaker (Fig. 34), which is accentuated with rippling horizontal lines that flow down from the apex opening, is a fine example of her consummate skill. Her raising of common household objects to the status of icons is a positive feminist expression in metalwork.

Betteridge is also a teacher. Through workshops, lectures and apprenticeships, she has taught two generations of Canadians. In a period when metalwork was ruled by modernism and devoid of embellishment, Betteridge went her own way, pushing metal to its malleable limits. Her most personal expression was a baroque-fantasy ice-cream cone of silver gilt, which encased family photographs (Plate 10). As Bronfman winner, Betteridge had the opportunity to put together a body of work, which she entitled *Reflections in Silver*. The collection toured eight major art galleries in Canada from 1981 to 1983.

Jewellery as beautiful ornament, such as Klocke's gold-cast brooch, dominated much of the seventies. Experiments with titanium and plastics, however, were leading edge. These were often flatter in appearance, more like graphic canvases.

A geometric approach to metal was beginning to challenge the prevailing organic forms of the sixties and early seventies. Rather than approaching metal as a carrier for a stone, metalsmiths were beginning to exploit the properties of metal itself.

By the end of the seventies, jewellers and craftspeople were exploring new materials and techniques, as Bersudsky had urged them to do a decade earlier. This would continue into the 1980s, when experimentation was at its peak. Canadian metalsmiths were also closely following, through books and craft magazines, the groundbreaking ideas of German, Dutch and English jewellers, including Klaus Bury, Emmy van Leersum, Gijs Bakker, Wendy Ramshaw, David Watkins, Susanna Heron and Caroline Broadhead. One of the "pieces" by Gijs Bakker was a mark left on the skin by a tightly drawn wire. While the Canadian public was not ready for such ideas, art jewellers were stimulated by this new jewellery movement.

Fig. 35. | S u e   P a r k e | headdress, 1986, dyed clothes pins, plastic-coated cable, wooden beads. Photo: Peter Hogan.

Fig. 36. | Theo Janson | Mask, 1981, copper, fabricated, patinated.

The 1980s:

Jewellery in Transition

In comparison with previous decades, in which amateurs had enjoyed learning about jewellery and hollowware more for personal pleasure than for financial gain, the majority of Canadian students emerging from college metal programs in the 1970s and 1980s intended to earn a living from their craft. Equipped with résumés and slide sheets, they approached galleries and stores to sell their work, or sought jobs as designers and bench workers with jewellery-manufacturing firms. Their training and determination translated into a more professional approach to exhibitions and catalogues and to their own work.

Diane Hanson and Betty Walton, graduates of George Brown College, both entered the production jewellery market with explorations in anodized aluminum. Hanson used felt markers to pattern individual sheets of aluminum, which she then cut into earrings and brooches. Her patterns had an immediacy of design and richness of colour variation (see Plate 11). Walton used reticulation to achieve surface textures in aluminum, which she then coloured and combined with silver. She also worked with delicately coloured aluminum rods (see Plate 12). The use of aluminum by both of these jewellers was part of a move toward the non-precious in jewellery.

Good as Gold

The prevailing attitude of the early eighties was that gold limited artistic expression: its colouring possibilities were narrow, its cost was prohibitive, and its ostentation restricted wearability. Even art jewellers who called themselves goldsmiths began to question the value of gold. The trend away from gold and toward other materials was brought home to Canadian jewellers in 1983 in an exhibition called *Good as Gold,* which was put on by the Smithsonian Institution in Washington, D.C., and travelled to the Craft Gallery at the Ontario Crafts Council, in Toronto. The show displayed the work of ninety Americans, who used everything from found objects to cornhusks and handmade paper.

Coinciding with this exhibition, the Ontario Crafts Council and MAG Ontario staged *Good as Gold: A Conference for Jewellers.* This was the first conference for art jewellers in Canada, and it attracted 125 participants from five provinces and four states. The keynote speaker was Ralph Turner, head of exhibitions at the British Crafts Council, in London, and co-founder of the Electrum Gallery. His slide lecture centered on the new British jewellery of Caroline Broadhead, Susanna Heron, Julia Manheim, David Watkins and Pierre Degen. Turner generated much controversy with his notion that traditional jewellery was dead and with his broadening of the term *jewellery* to include pieces such as Pierre Degen's ten-foot-high ladder sculptures. James Evans provided a survey of the Canadian scene, which he declared to be blessed with technically good jewellery that lacked sufficient gallery exposure; Bruce Metcalf offered an impressive slide presentation on the "New Aesthetics;" Neil Carrick Aird gave a talk on the presentation of ideas to clients; David LaPlantz demonstrated his latest work in aluminum; and Michael Lieber demonstrated metal lamination. There was also a panel discussion on health hazards — one of the first to warn artists about the dangers of cadmium solders, lead and asbestos.

In response to the *Good as Gold* exhibition and the British exhibition *Jewellery Redefined,* Suzann Greenaway, at Prime Canadian Crafts in Toronto, staged *Jewellery in Transition,* a selection of non-precious multi-media jewellery. The show provided proof that alternative jewellery could be beautiful, biting and fun. Kai Chan tied red dogwood branches together with coloured silk threads and shaped them into natural neckpieces and bracelets; James Evans turned slate roof tiles into brooches; and Richard Karpyshin affixed red, enamel "X" pins onto a series of black-and-white photographs of torsos (Plate 13). But the most politically charged piece at the exhibition belonged to David Didur. In his neckpiece *Medal for Dishonour* (Plate 14), Didur offered a scathing indictment of American cruise-missile testing in Canada. The piece was made up of a short fuse, firecrackers and matches, all interwoven with "threads of credibility," and from it dangled a pendant silhouette of the United States.

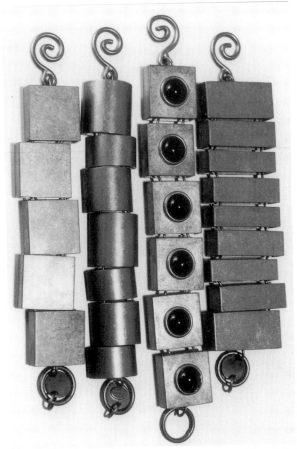

Fig. 37. | M a r t h a S t u r d y | metal bracelets, 1980s. Photo: Dan Couto.

Fig. 39. [A n d r e w   G o s s] earring, 1983, polyester, paper, sterling silver, steel, fabricated, laminated, 9 x 1.2 cm. Photo: Jeremy Jones.

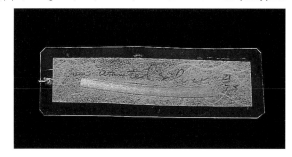

The eighties featured several forays into performance art that incorporated jewellery. For the show *Headdresses and Breastplates,* held at the Toronto jewellery gallery Harhay & McKay, a dancer enthralled onlookers by interpreting the jewellery in movement. Sue Parke's headdress (Fig. 35), made of everyday clothespins arranged into a crown, was a dramatic contribution to the show.

A sense of the theatrical was also present in a series of masks made by Theo Janson, of Toronto, who received fine arts training at the University of Florida. Janson, whose previous work had often involved figurative cutouts, enjoyed the mystery and drama of concealment. One mask, made of patinated copper and coloured with theatre gels, had a broken and overlapping surface that suggested a Janus-face (Fig. 36). Some were designed to be carried on sticks and others became neckpieces.

In Montreal, Madeleine Dansereau planned an experimental course on adornment for the theatre at the École de Joaillerie et de Métaux d'Art. She invited two professors to lecture on theatre history and scenography. They chose the Bertolt Brecht play *The Life of Galileo* for its relevance to contemporary life. The third-act ball scene gave students the occasion to create masks and other adornment in paper. To Dansereau, the experience resulted in a lasting lesson in the relationship between the body and adornment.

As part of the *Good as Gold* conference, Monica Harhay, a graduate of the metal program at the Sheridan College School of Design, chaired a fashion show called *Parallel Lines: Fashion Meets Jewellery.* The show helped to forge stronger ties between Toronto's clothing designers and jewellers. Fashion designers, however, have always considered jewellery as "accessory," to which Montreal jeweller Georges Schwartz has the ready retort: "If I sell a brooch for $35,000, the clothing is the accessory."

Vogue magazine has shown the work of many Canadian jewellery designers, but none more than that of Martha Sturdy, of Vancouver. With a background in sculpture, Sturdy gave the fashion-jewellery market a jolt when she introduced her large, bold earrings, bracelets and rings, first of metal and then of cast resins in strong colours. Her jewellery was clearly not for the timid. Its stark geometric forms in unit constructions stood out in the showcase and on the wearer (see Fig. 37). Sturdy began to develop a reputation for her work, though more abroad than in Canada. She established a studio and worked diligently at marketing to achieve her success in the competitive fashion field. But in the nineties, in response to the vicissitudes of fashion, Sturdy would turn to designing functional objects. She considers all of her work — individually assembled pieces, polished and finished by hand — to be modern art.

Kim Snyder, a graduate of Sheridan College School of Design and the OCA, turned to acrylics in the eighties and also became a favourite in the fashion pages. In *Acrylic is a Plastic Medium,* a 1987 technical paper, Snyder discussed small-scale applications of acrylics. His bracelet *Weeds in Stream* is a good example of his complex approach to the medium (Fig. 38). Snyder carved the piece internally, added polyester resin, and then laminated with metallic powder. For a time, before returning to his roots in precious metals, Snyder worked creatively to transform humble materials into high-quality jewellery.

Light sticks (cyalume rods) provided a bright alternative to the gleam of gemstones for Paul Leathers, of Winnipeg (see Plate 15). The light sticks, when bent, would blend two chemicals, resulting in a cool, extra-terrestrial glow that would last for about twelve hours. Leathers, a graduate of NSCAD, incorporated them into sterling silver brooches with finely textured surfaces.

The attraction of alternative materials, such as plastics, paper and found objects, was more than just the result of artists opting for cheaper supplies when the price of gold and silver rose in the early eighties. Jewellery had always been primarily considered as ornament for the body, and was often used as a symbol of engagement, marriage, graduation, association or wealth. But, beginning in the Netherlands in the mid-sixties, and in England in the seventies, a radical questioning began to push the concept of jewellery to its limits: Must jewellery be worn, or could it stand on its own, as sculpture? Was the expression of ideas more important than the object created? Was it not best to work in non-precious materials accessible to all members of society?

In 1983, concerned with how materials convey ideas, Canadian jeweller James Evans incorporated words on paper into his jewellery. According to Evans, "the words become the jewellery." Similarly, Andrew Goss, a graduate of the University of Toronto and George Brown College, encased a thin strip of silver in polyester, with the written quip: "you wanted silver" (Fig. 39). The earring offered a flash of silver, but, more importantly, offered you Goss's opinion that the idea is more important than the material. This kind of provocative jewellery appealed to many who liked testing limits.

On the momentum of the *Good as Gold* conference, MAG Ontario, in collaboration with the Ontario Crafts Council, decided it was ready to host the 1985 SNAG Conference. It was a heady, exhausting time for the organizers, who chose the theme "An International Gathering." The intent was to introduce the predominantly American membership to both Canadian and European jewellers. In design, most Canadian jewellers regarded American jewellery of the early eighties as too big, too funky, too assembled and too caught up in personal expression. Canadian jewellers preferred the work of the Dutch, German, and British jewellers, which they felt was more pared down and deliberate in its simplicity. The conference provoked much discussion and soul searching about the direction of Canadian art jewellery.

Paul Derrez, of Gallerie Ra, in Amsterdam, spoke about his commitment to a particular jewellery aesthetic that embraced non-precious materials and new forms for jewellery. Helen Drutt, a gallery owner from Philadelphia, related her involvement with contemporary jewellery; and Carole Hanks, then an art historian at Sheridan College, presented the work of Canadian jewellers. But the high point of the conference was a presentation by Otto Künzli, who questioned the role of gold, and, by inference, the role of the goldsmith in our society. His presentation culminated with a slide he had prepared especially for SNAG. A piece of gold sheet was mounted in place of the transparency, and when the slide came up, of course, nothing appeared on the screen. In effect, Künzli was implying that it is better to see good design and colourful images through a plastic transparency than to be blinded by a preoccupation with precious metal.

Canadian Directions

There was a real dynamism in many areas of the country in the 1980s, and it was generally linked with strong schools. The jewellery emanating from NSCAD and its graduates was particularly identifiable, both for its fine craftsmanship and its minimal design sensibility. In jurying *Profile 81* for the Nova Scotia Designer Crafts Council, Lois E. Betteridge credited the "influences of past and present staff strengths at NSCAD" for the innovative metalwork submitted.

Martha Glenny, a graduate of George Brown College, received her bachelor of fine arts from NSCAD in 1984 and has exhibited perfectly crafted, thoughtful work ever since. In her exhibits, Glenny likes to use visual puns. In her 1984 exhibit, *Souvenirs/le souvenir,* Glenny contrasted her perceptions of the Niagara Falls in which she grew up with the tourist's perception of Niagara Falls. In her 1986 exhibit, *Memoranda,* souvenirs played a major role again. For a piece called *Entry Charm* (Plate 16), she mounted such keepsakes as cancelled Paris Metro tickets and museum tickets onto a bracelet. The laminated ephemera of her trip thus became as precious as her memories. Glenny has continued to use laminated paper, and she often incorporates maps, for both their visual appeal and as references to geography and culture. Her 1992 pin *Taking it to the Bank?* (Fig. 40), featuring four laminated fish and a classical bank facade with a gold dollar sign, all suspended from a partial map of Newfoundland, is among few pieces in Canadian metalwork that offer such strong political commentary.

Jude Ortiz, a graduate of NSCAD and George Brown College, also used her jewellery to communicate specific messages. In a 1987 exhibit entitled *The Essence is Water,* Ortiz raised her concerns about water as a precious resource. Because jewellers usually consider gold and emeralds as our most precious commodities, Ortiz's plea was especially poignant. A series of pins entitled *In the Beginning* (Fig. 41) suggested, in a very formal way, that there was a balance of the forces of nature before human intervention. In the program for the exhibit, Ortiz asked poetic, probing questions about pollution and natural resources.

Fig. 40. Martha Glenny Taking it to the Bank? (brooch), 1992, 14-karat yellow gold, laminated paper, fabricated, 5 x 7 cm.

Fig. 41. Jude Ortiz from her In the Beginning series (brooches), 1987, 14-karat gold, sterling silver, ebony.

Fig. 42. Nora Goreham Birth of Agate (box), 1973, sterling silver, Nova Scotia agate.

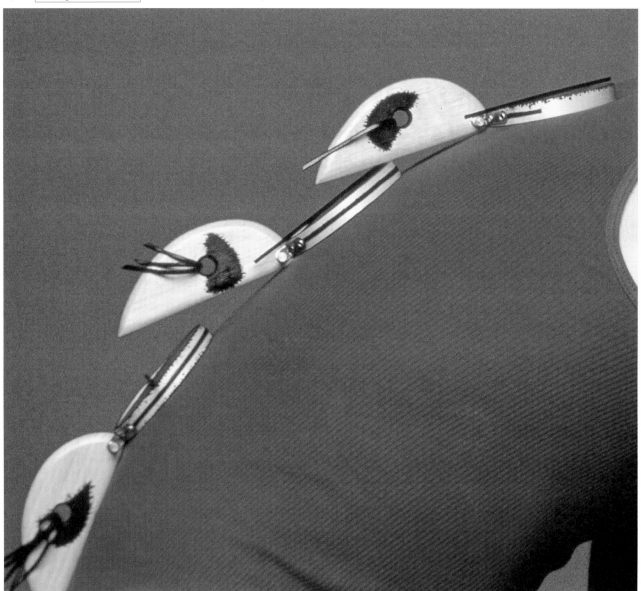

62

In 1984, MAG Nova Scotia mounted a retrospective exhibition in honour of such dedicated members as Andy and Morna Anderson, Ellis Roulston, Jean Mosher and Clifford Brown, each of whom had been with the guild for many years. The work exhibited spanned decades of design styles and was very different from what was coming out of NSCAD at the time. The exhibition demonstrated a long tradition of work with precious metals and stones, and featured the beautiful Nova Scotia agate designs of Nora Goreham (see Fig. 42).

In Alberta, three exhibitions focussed on jewellery as body ornament. The Alberta College of Art gallery presented *Bodywork: A Selection of Canadian Jewellery,* in 1986, and the Muttart Gallery staged *For the Body,* in 1988, and *On Body Ornamentation,* in 1989. For the last of these, the public was invited to attend "adorned and decorated." The exhibitors (and the public) displayed work in a myriad of materials, from electronic parts to dead fish. Inspired by whales, Morgan Bristol, a student at the Alberta College of Art, used wood, leather and paint to create jewellery to be worn on the back (Fig. 43).

Alberta College of Art graduate Jackie Anderson became known during the eighties both for her use of unusual materials and for her evocation of place. In her presentation, Anderson was inspired by commercial signs and architectural models. In *Eamons* (Plate 17), a segment of checkerboard floor and a background reminiscent of the period were used as a display stand for a large brooch. The brooch was constructed — in sterling silver, diamond, amethyst, acrylic and polyester resin — using design elements of a sign that Anderson had photographed.

Sheridan College graduates also produced notable work. In 1980, Maureen Wilson and Sherry Otterway joined with metal instructor Bev de Jong to mount an exhibition called *Metalmorphics.* As the title implied, the concept was to show changes in the field of metalwork. The three artists used metal to express very personal ideas. De Jong, who attended the Alberta College of Art and Cranbrook Academy, showed a large bronze mirror of wonderful complexity entitled *Self Portrait* (Fig. 44). The piece, incorporating an ebony torso of a helmeted woman on the reverse, handmade chain mail, and a photo-etched self portrait, was an expression of de Jong's interest in women's relationship with metal's history including its use in battle. One juror called it a masterpiece. The mirror's strong, hand-raised form, with rich surface treatment and personal imagery, also pointed to the changes that were occurring in Canadian metal objects. The functional, unadorned hollowware of the 1950s was being challenged by such highly decorated personal objects.

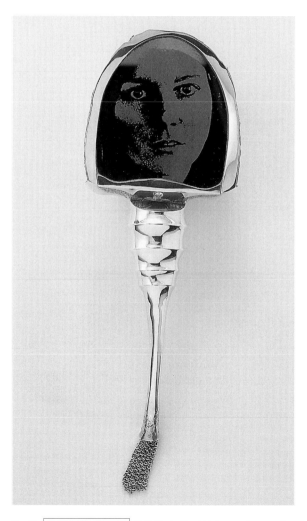

Fig. 44. Bev de Jong Self Portrait, 1980, bronze, ebony, sterling silver chain mail, raised handle, photo-etched image, reticulated, inlaid, 42 x 15 x 5 cm. Photo: Bernard de Jong.

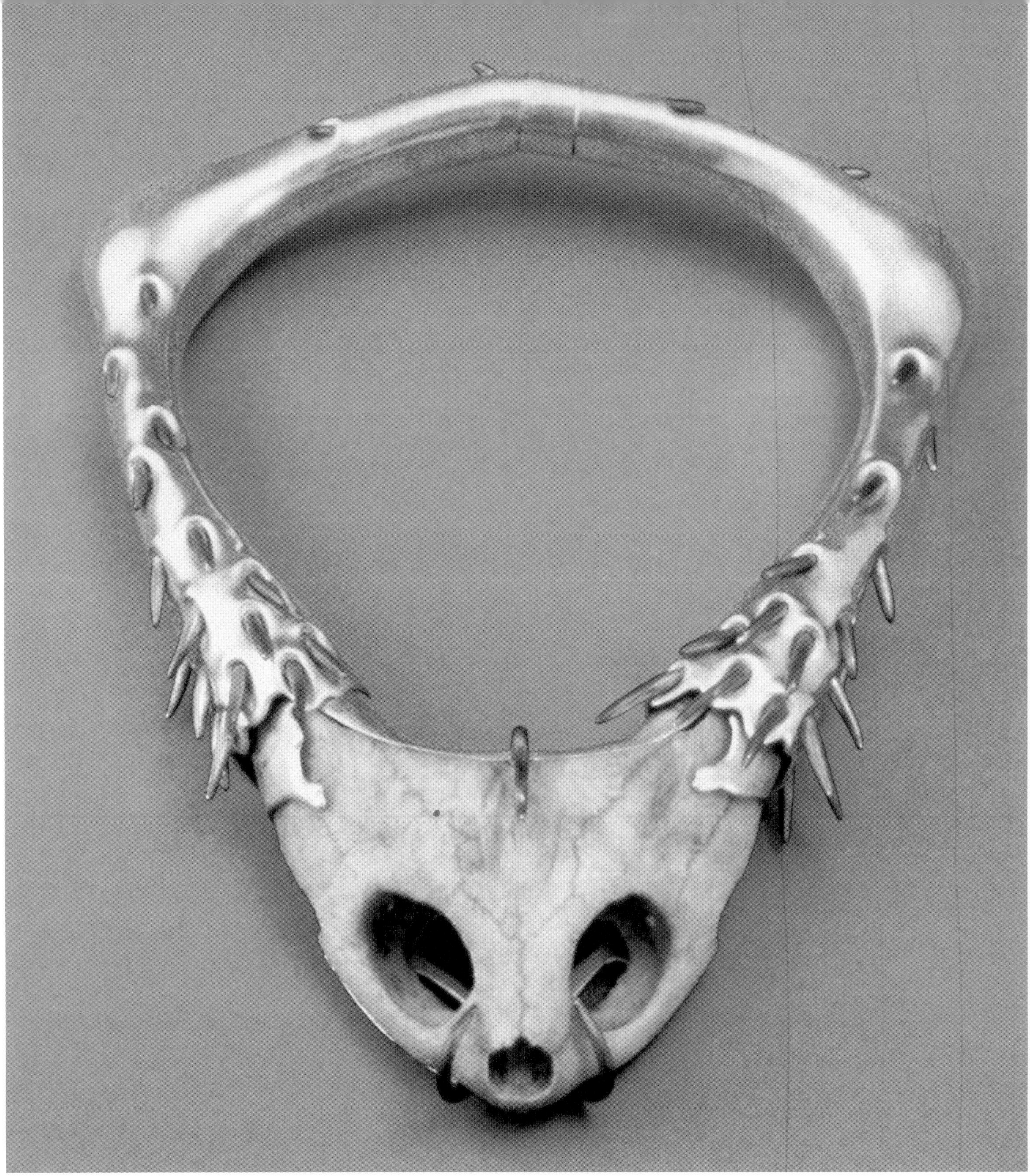

Fig. 45. | Sherry Otterway | When All Else Fails (neckpiece), 1980, sterling silver, copper, turtle skull, fabricated. Photo: Ben Hogan.

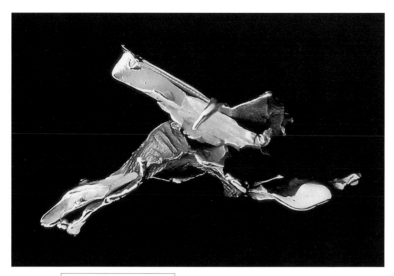

Maureen Wilson, of British Columbia, used triangular and pyramidal shapes to relate cosmic philosophies of numerology and myth. With coloured theatre gels and found objects, her brooches evoked images of space. The surfaces were intricate, with etched lines, gemstones and bits of texture. Like de Jong, Wilson was sharing something deeply personal.

Sherry Otterway's integration of a turtle skull into a neckpiece provoked a strong reaction from gallery goers (Fig. 45). Aside from the skull, copper hairs on the neckpiece made it look rather uncomfortable. Otterway's work was somewhat threatening. "I'm taking out my aggressions in my work," she explained, "It can be vicious, but with people I'm quite peaceful." Otterway challenged jewellery's conventional ideas of beauty, and posited her own aesthetic. To some it seemed self-indulgent, but to others it heralded a needed change.

In Montreal, the work of Claude Loranger and Louis-Jacques Suzor, both of whom studied at the École de Joaillerie et de Métaux d'Art, revealed differing metal sensibilities. Loranger explored organic forms in cast silver and gold. Loaded with emotion, his patinated brooches captured the dark side of nature and continued the strong three-dimensional approach of much Quebec jewellery (for an example, see Fig. 46). But a cooler, more architectural approach to metal and stones distinguished the brooches of Suzor (see Fig. 47)

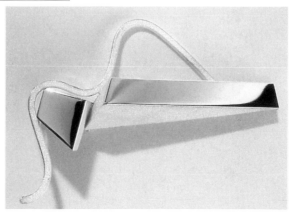

Fig. 48. **Maurice Brault** ring, 1976, 18-karat yellow gold, diamonds.

Fig. 49. **Maurice Brault** brooch, 1985, marbled wood, sterling silver.

Fig. 50. **Peter Lawrence** three brooches, 1985, sterling silver, straw, 10-karat gold, fabricated, oxidized, 6 x 5 cm., 7 x 4 cm., 7 x 4 cm.

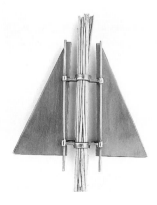

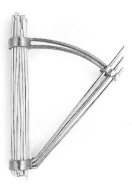

Fig. 51. | Martha Glenny | brooch, 1984, sterling silver, gold, diamonds, cobalite in quartzite, fabricated. Photo: Jeremy Jones.

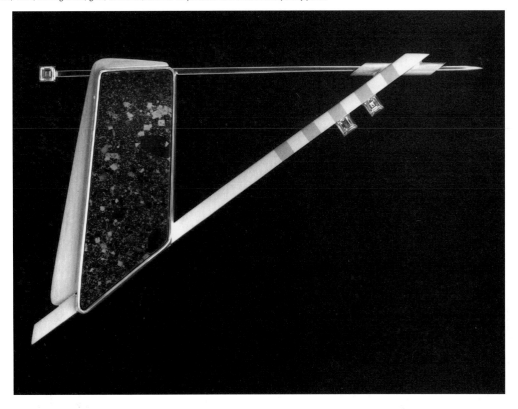

New directions were also seen among established jewellers. Maurice Brault, of Montreal, graduated from the École des Beaux-Arts (in Montreal) in 1951, and from the École Supérieure d'Architecture et des Arts Décoratifs de l'Abbaye de la Cambré (in Brussels) in 1955. He then apprenticed in Norway. Brault participated in numerous exhibitions and received many awards, including an honourable mention at the Canadian Pavilion of the *Universal and International Exhibition* in Brussels in 1958. His 1970s work — exhibited at the store of Gabriel Lucas in Montreal — showed wit with diamonds and gold. His mailbox ring (Fig. 48), for example, hinged open to reveal a diamond safely tucked inside. In 1982, Brault went to Italy and rediscovered an old Turkish marbling technique called Ebru. Using marbled silk and wood with silver, he created a series of neckpieces and brooches (an example is shown in Fig. 49), which he exhibited in Italy and at Art Wear (Robert Lee Morris's jewellery gallery in New York City).

Influences

The design influences of the eighties ranged from minimalism to hard-edged geometric formalism to postmodernism. Perhaps the most minimalist show of all was MAG Ontario's *The Medium is Metal 1984,* held at Prime Canadian Crafts Gallery. Jurors Christian Gaudernack, Neil Carrick Aird and Carol Rapp chose from two hundred pieces that emanated from across Canada. The jury favoured innovative design and materials. Peter Lawrence showed a series of brooches in oxidized sterling silver with straw (Fig. 50); Oksana Kit and Diane Hanson showed work in anodized aluminum; Akira Ikegami showed brooches of gold-plated brass, gold, shakudo and acrylic; Heike Raschl-Labrecque submitted anodized titanium, oxidized copper and rubber; and Joanne Critchley Browne showed work in sterling silver, gold, pearl and moose antler.

Martha Glenny's clean, angular brooch of silver, gold, diamonds, and cobalite in quartzite (Fig. 51) took top honours. Its unusual pin closure was especially interesting; instead of being hidden behind the brooch, this pin stem worked as part of the design.

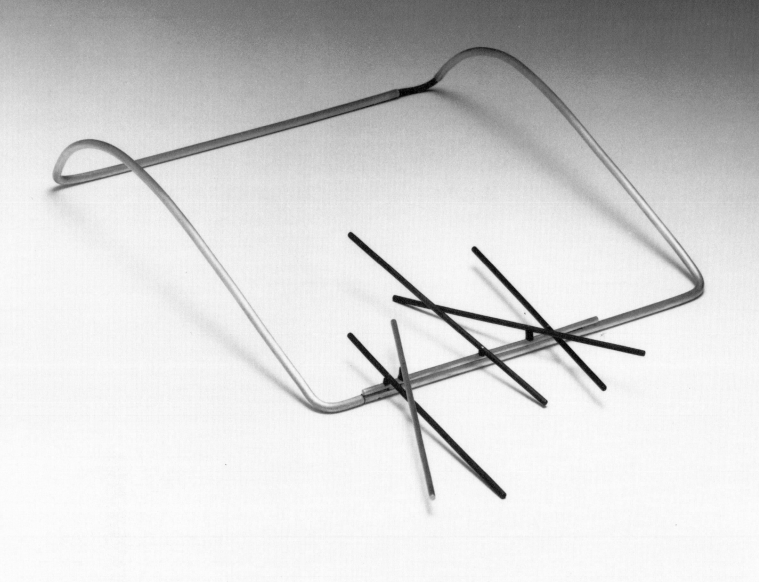

Fig. 52. | Heike Raschl-Labrecque | neckpiece with removable brooch, 1985, sterling silver, shakudo, rubber, fabricated, 26 x 19 cm. Photo: Jeremy Jones.

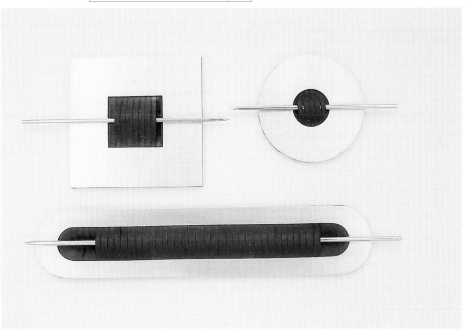

Some metalsmiths who worked in a more traditional aesthetic were bruised by the show's rejection of the traditional in favour of minimalism. But the struggle between tradition and innovation at juried shows has often been bitter.

Heike Raschl-Labrecque, who attended OCA and George Brown College, began winning awards in 1985 for her minimalist jewellery. Her design sensibility was characterized by a softly geometric neck-piece with a removable brooch of angled shakudo rods (Fig. 52). A rubber insert at the back of the neckpiece allowed for flexibility without detracting from the form. Raschl-Labrecque's elegant use of black rubber, when most of the world associated it with tire manufacturing, was a bold move. In one set of brooches (Fig. 53), rubber is encased in silver forms that attach to the wearer's clothing by needles that pierce the rubber. Quebec jeweller Lise Fortin also worked with flat geometric forms. Her brooch of tumbling square forms (Fig. 54) proved that the geometric approach to design need not be boring.

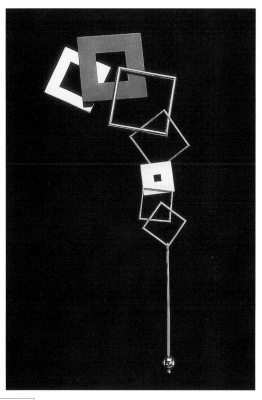

Fig. 54. | Lise Fortin | brooch, 1986, sterling silver, ebony, 10 x 20 cm. Photo: Jeremy Jones.

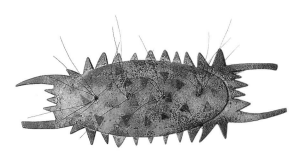

Along with the minimalist aesthetic came the colour boom. Where shiny metals had glittered against black velvet in the fifties and sixties, exhibitions in the mid-eighties featured patinated greens and reds against handmade paper. MAG Ontario's fortieth anniversary was celebrated with a show entitled *The Medium is Metal: the Theme is Colour.* The founders would have been amazed at the range of colours metal had taken on since 1946. Along with strong varied hues of aluminum were pink-brown tantalum, purple titanium, red, green and yellow epoxy resin, and blue-green patinated brass and copper, as well as the muted tones of niobium and bright acrylics and enamels. One reviewer praised a brooch by David McAleese and Alison Wiggins, made with vitrolite and jasper, as making the best use of colour. Oksana Kit and Diane Hanson's orange-patterned wallpiece with Velcro-attached shapes (Plate 18) also scored well. According to the jury, "The most successful entries demonstrated a restraint in the use of colour and a sensitivity to its ability to enhance the form and content of a piece." Delicately shaded work, like that of OCA graduate Shayne Kjertinge, accentuated the play between the formal elements (Plate 19).

With the colour craze of the eighties came an interest in Japanese metalsmithing techniques, which were first studied closely in the 1970s by Gene Pijanowski and Hiroko Sato Pijanowski of the United States. Akira Ikegami, a teaching master at George Brown College whose fine arts training was in Japan, promoted the use of aluminum, refractory metals and traditional Japanese techniques (Plate 20). The alloys *shakudo* (gold and silver) and *shibuichi* (silver and copper), and *mokume-gane,* a wood-grained metal effect achieved through the fusion and carving of various coloured metals, were frequently seen in exhibition work. These metals provided rich colours, from reddish brown to silver gray and velvet black.

Laminations of various coloured metals were also highly regarded by metalsmiths. The simplest laminations were made by soldering together silver and copper rods and then rolling them out to achieve a striped effect. More complex laminations involved twisting of the metals until they formed repeat patterns such as those in the work of Kye-yeon Son (Fig. 62).

Other popular eighties techniques included cold gilding with metal leaf and colouring with chemicals. These were easier processes to command, and several technical books came out during the eighties that enabled jewellers and metalsmiths to experiment in the studio.

As well as revealing the strong trend toward colour, MAG Ontario's shows in the eighties reaped the benefits of extensive fundraising activities. Serious efforts at seeking prize money resulted in awards being handed out in a larger number of categories. Along with the best-in-show and design awards, there was now an award for the best piece of production jewellery. Depending on the theme of the show, awards were also given for casting, enamelling, sculpture and hollowware.

The production jewellery award was donated by Burkhardt Jewellers, of Toronto, a company that offered a model for emerging jewellers to follow. As a manufacturing jeweller, Burkhardt began a line of contemporary earrings and bracelets in sterling silver in the 1970s. The company hired recent college graduates to design and make this line, giving them experience with manufacturing techniques and buyers. In retrospect, the influence of these educated designers is readily apparent in Burkhardt's modern silver jewellery. Where production jewellery was once dismissed as substandard and uninspired, it began to command a new respect in the art jewellery community.

Buoyed by the success of its previous conferences, MAG Ontario reached out again in 1987 and invited Canadian jewellers and metalsmiths to *A Closer Look*. The conference speakers — Brigitte Clavette from New Brunswick, Judith Anderson from Nova Scotia, Lise Fortin from Quebec, Alison Parsons from Ontario and David Rice from Winnipeg — presented strong visual records of what was happening in the various regions. The exhibition accompanying the conference featured an award-winning brooch by Brenda Bear Epp, which was made with patinated brass and polar bear hair (Fig. 55). Brigitte Clavette showed her *Fly Brooch,* of sterling silver, onyx and deer hair; Brooke Baillie's brooch presented bears as domesticated targets (Plate 21); and Sabine Mittermayer took best-in-show with was a long sterling silver pin that balanced a round, natural stone against a smooth needle form (Fig. 56). In *Metalsmith* magazine, Carole Hanks described the work as portraying "city sophistication locked into a dialogue with nature."

As in 1983, the participants enjoyed the opportunity to meet and to see each other's work. MAG Ontario found new members in other provinces and encouraged more interaction and reporting of local events in its publication. Everyone was surprised at the number of talented metalsmiths who were busy creating in isolation all across the country, thoughtfully confronting personal, environmental and social issues in their daily work. Stephen Inglis, Director of Research of the

71

Fig. 56. Sabine Mittermayer   pin, 1987, sterling silver, stone, 31 x 4 cm. Photo: Jeremy Jones.

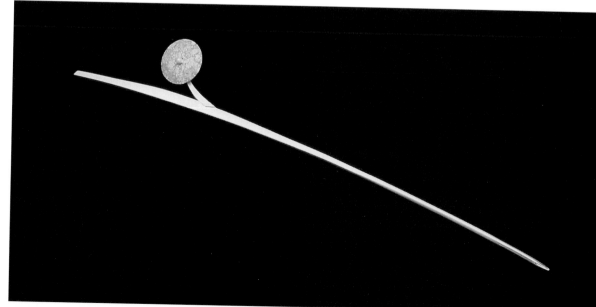

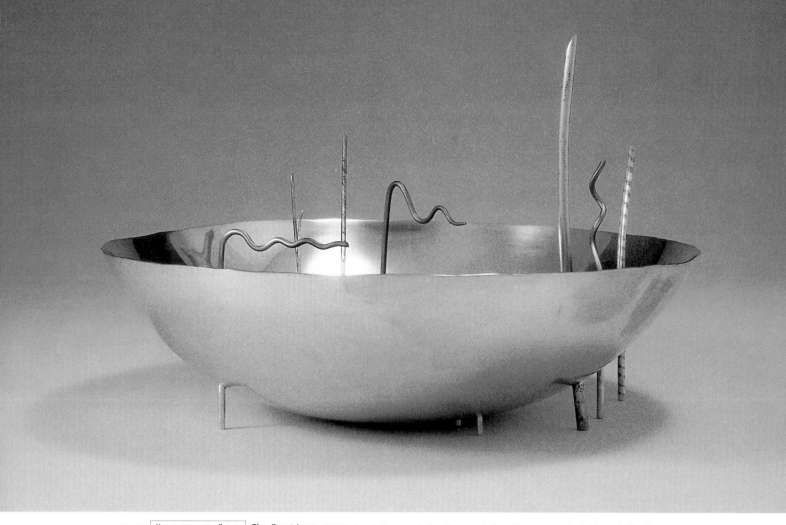

Fig. 57. **Kye-yeon Son** The Great Love, 1987, heat treated copper, sterling silver, nickel silver, 24-karat gold, raised, fabricated, 22 x 22 x 12.5 cm.

Museum of Civilization, addressed this isolation in his keynote address, in which he reminded his audience that isolation for the craftsperson is not only physical, it is also societal, for craft is even isolated within the arts. Both the public's perception of craft as "handicraft" and the institutional structures that restricted and categorized the arts rendered craft a poor cousin. Inglis posited a reassessment of craft within a more anthropological framework. Inglis asserted that crafts provide an opportunity to study the techniques and work of other cultures, past and present, and help to define one's sense of place — "a persistent issue in Canada."

Brenda Bear Epp's work in the eighties addressed the search for Canadian identity. Jurors were easily won over by her patinated pointy brooches with brightly coloured moose hair. Influenced by her background in theatre, Epp's presentations always had a dramatic element. Her scarab pins, commissioned by the Ontario Government as a gift to the Royal Ontario Museum (Plate 22), were displayed on a tall wood-and-metal stand. The result was very sophisticated. Its art brut approach to jewellery was unlike anyone else's.

Hollowware

Contemporary Canadian Hollowware, a curated exhibition, was held at the Ontario Crafts Council in 1986. The exhibition focussed much discussion on the state of raised vessels and sculptural forms, and the plight of the silversmith. Although there was ongoing debate at SNAG conferences in the eighties about whether or not hollowware could be sculpture, this exhibition came down firmly on the side of function. The five participants exhibited a wide range of approaches to metal. Kye-yeon Son, a graduate of Indiana University and apprentice with Lois E. Betteridge, showed raised shallow bowls with tangential pieces and standards. One of these, with a crossing of married metal rods, was entitled *The Great Love* (Fig. 57). It was exciting, and quietly colourful. Michael Surman, British born and trained, exhibited a traditional sterling silver wine cooler with chased fluting. It was a perfectly executed repetition of a classic form. Paula Letki showed large spun bowls, which were etched and patinated, and embedded with fine silver wire. Each bowl sat at an off angle to a pear-wood base. Michael Letki exhibited a tall, fabricated aluminum clock of clean linear design. Sheridan College graduate Zahava Lambert showed copper vessels with exuberant collars accented in fused silver.

But despite this exhibition, function began to lose ground to sculpture in the eighties. Not only were many smiths being trained in sculpture, but the postmodern period was beginning to influence their attitudes. The Scandinavian aesthetic, which had been adored for much of the century, could not satisfy the demand for innovative ideas, materials and techniques. Anne Barros, a Toronto silversmith, turned to tin-plated steel, which she decorated with bright, mottled colours (Plate 23). Other smiths patinated their hollowware explorations.

Although there were more metalsmiths in the eighties, there was less hollowware in evidence than in the fifties. Where a good portion of shows in the fifties was dedicated to coffee sets, boxes and bowls, MAG shows in the eighties often lamented the lack of objects submitted. In general, the shows reflected the 1980s market, which was about ninety percent jewellery and ten percent hollowware and flatware. The monopoly of stainless steel in the hollowware/flatware market was hard on the individual silversmith; it was impossible to compete with the prices of manufactured stainless steel.

Fortunately, postmodernism's interest in architectural metalwork and patinated vessels promoted work on a larger scale. One artist who took advantage of this was Ontario's David Didur, who turned from jewellery to larger installations with his company, Standing Metal Works. Didur collaborated with architects and other artists to make clock faces, signage and railings. He also took on a commission to design "deviant surgical tools" for David Cronenberg's film *Dead Ringers.* For himself, he made patinated copper vessels that doubled as sculpture. *New Moon in Rimouski* (Plate 24) exhibited a flare that was unusual in Canadian hollowware. Its spiralling form and attached taper gestured away from complete containment. Didur, who studied at NSCAD, strongly believes that craft must respond creatively to today's world, and that the craftsperson should receive due recompense for his or her response.

Enamelling

With the advent of the Canadian Biennials of Enamel in Laval, Quebec, in 1981, 1983 and 1985, and with the formation of the Corporation des Émailleurs du Québec, there has been renewed interest in this most demanding "art of fire." *L'Émail au Québec 1949–1989,* an exhibition curated by Lise Larochelle-Roy in 1989, featured the fine work done by Marcel Dupond, Jean-Jacques Spénard, Francois Desrochers, Monique Drolet-Coté, Richard Thériault and others in Quebec after the Second World War (this exhibition is documented in the book *L'Émail au Quebec*).

Enamellists are often considered part of the metal community in Canada, but they also belong to the glass and ceramic communities. With their own guilds, they have gained respect on the international scene, and Canadian enamellists now participate in juried and invitational exhibitions in the United States, France, Germany, Spain and Japan.

Fay Rooke, of Burlington, Ontario, has been a teacher and leader in enamelling since the seventies and enjoys an international reputation. In her work, she explores highly personal themes. Her collection *Passages (1984–1987)* emanated from the challenges and rewards of her earlier body of work, *Freedoms and Choices (1980–1984)*. According to Rooke, the piece *Autumn Garden Passage* (Plate 25) presents "that fleeting last day when the colours that are left are in the wet puddles . . . and the beauty of it all will last in spite of us." Rooke's distinction in the enamel community comes not only from her combination of enamelling techniques but also from the unusual shapes of her raised and pierced copper forms, which she hand polishes in the traditional way.

A. Alan Perkins has been enamelling master at George Brown College since 1968. Perkins considers himself an "ink junkie." With a background in architectural drawing, he explores, in large format, ideas of line and space. There is also an underlying commentary about architecture's relationship with history and nature. His *Massey Hall 1894* façade (Plate 26), one of a group of thirty-five enamels, entitled *Early Ontario Series,* directs attention to the preservation of our heritage. Perkins's overglaze drawings on porcelain enamel, sometimes combined with photo collage, are appealing for their straightforward use of the medium. His approach has secured him large-scale corporate commissions and international renown.

James Doran, of Winnipeg, brings a very different sensibility to his enamelling. Influenced by the surrealism of René Magritte, his enamelled assemblages are of everyday objects realistically grouped according to his intention. So realistic are his enamel tableaux that when *Check Mate* (Plate 27) was exhibited in Montreal, a member of the cleaning staff was heard mumbling sotto voce about the lack of respect some people had for the art on display. When the director looked up, the employee was waving one of the enamel-on-copper matches, saying, "Look where those people leave their ashtrays!" With humour, Doran points out the foibles of contemporary society.

Exhibitions

The eighties proved a fertile period for jewellery and metal exhibitions, not only in Canada but also abroad. Influential international publications, including *Gold + Silber* and *Art Aurea,* printed photographs and articles about Canadian jewellery, and important exhibitions and books featured Canadian artists. MAG Ontario exhibited in Schwabish-Gmund, Germany, as part of a provincial cultural exchange, and *Five Canadian Jewellers,* an invitational exhibition, travelled in Australia.

The first Canadian jewellers to exhibit at Electrum Gallery, the foremost contemporary jewellery gallery in England, were Kai Chan, James Evans and Louis Tortell. Their 1985 show revealed a common preference for non-precious materials that allowed them greater freedom to express ideas and made their work more accessible to the public. Chan, a graduate in interior design at OCA, explored jewellery as wearable art using natural materials like branches and reeds. His awareness of the body and its relationship with the environment and his fearlessness in working on a large scale led to work of great integrity. Although Chan had no formal training in jewellery, international jewellery books often pointed to him as representative of Canada. He had two solo shows during the eighties at Gallerie Ra, in Amsterdam. His armbands of palm leaves and silk (Plate 28) clearly suited the feeling of the times that jewellery was breaking out of its restrictive shell.

The work of James Evans, who studied at George Brown College and NSCAD, exemplified the fractious days in the eighties when ideas and minimal forms battled against traditional jewellery. Evans showed painted steel forms at Electrum (Fig. 58). They reflected his opinion that jewellery should engage the wearer and communicate ideas of egalitarianism and form. Evans was to pursue this point of view further in a 1985 exhibition entitled *Brooching Certain Subjects,* which was held at the State Art and Crafts Museum in Trondheim, Norway.

Visitors to the gallery found thin painted rods stacked against the walls. Soon people were being pinned together — shoulder to arm, back to back — and the concept of jewellery was pushed to include interpersonal activity. Evans's penchant for language led him to do much critical writing in international publications and to become a good ambassador for Canadian jewellery during the eighties. His visits to European galleries and his contact with European artists opened the door to many exhibitions and exchanges.

Fig. 58. │ J a m e s   E v a n s │ set of seven brooches, 1985, stainless steel, paint, fabricated, each 5 cm. in diameter. Photo: Jeremy Jones.

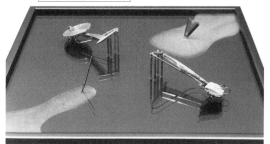

Louis Tortell, a graduate of Sheridan College School of Design, worked in the early eighties in precious metals and stones, often with articulated parts and a surface intricacy that reflected the complex cityscape of his native Malta. *Looking for My Heel,* which won MAG Ontario's Steel Trophy in 1981, was a set piece of two pins in a framed environment (Fig. 59). He later produced a series of armpieces made of textured stainless steel and hand-painted silk (Plate 29), which was exhibited at the Electrum Gallery, in London. The silk was used to hold the bracelet tight to the arm, and in the metal portions, Tortell experimented with various coloured alloys for contrast. Opportunities with international exhibitions and catalogues spurred him to show more adventurous work.

In 1988, Don Gidley and Paula Letki curated a show of eighteen Ontario jewellers, entitled *Embellished Elements.* The show travelled to the Electrum Gallery and to the Royal Canadian Academy in Toronto. At Electrum, alongside some of the world's most innovative contemporary jewellery, the show was decidedly middle of the road. However, the acrylic brooches of David McAleese and Alison Wiggins showed experimentation with both new forms and a new material. These playful acrylic cutouts, which they called *Biomorphs* (see Fig. 60), were a mixture of coloured geometric shapes inlaid in speckled protozoan forms. As with their previous experimentation with titanium, these brooches were a fresh response to the challenge of a new material.

In Montreal, Claudette Hardy-Pilon's solo exhibition at Galerie Jocelyne Gobeil, in 1987, revealed important changes in her work. Showing the influence of her fascination with oriental art, Hardy-Pilon used mostly copper-based metals and rusted scrap iron, with a flash of gold, in strong simple forms. *In Collier* (Fig. 61), she put together lengths of aluminum tubing, strands of rubber and a large, rusted steel disc. This made for a subdued colour palette with richly textured surfaces.

76

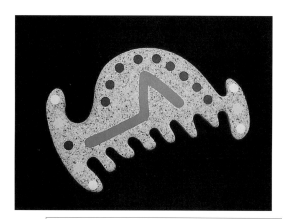

Fig. 60. David McAleese and Alison Wiggins Micromorphic #3 (brooch), 1987, acrylic, fabricated, inlayed, 12 x 8 x 0.5 cm. Photo: Jeremy Jones.

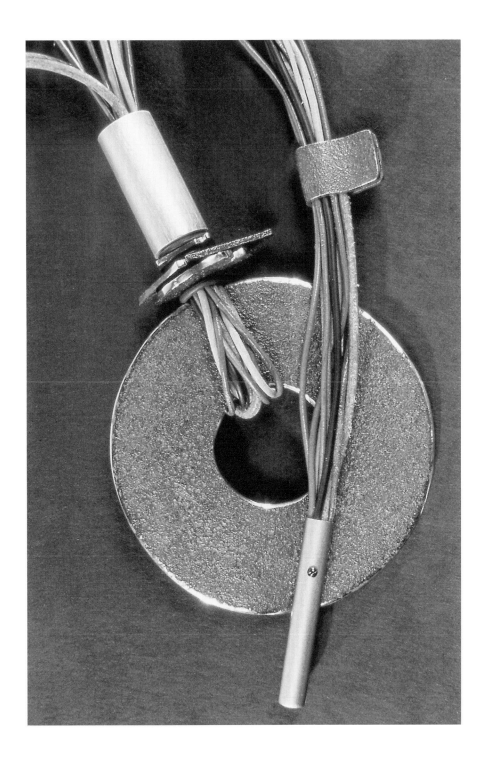

Fig. 61. Claudette Hardy-Pilon Collier, 1987, steel, aluminum, leather, rubber, fabricated.

Fig. 62. ⸺ K y e - y e o n   S o n ⸺ Salt and Pepper, 1988, sterling silver, nickel silver, new gold, 12 cm. high. Photo: Jeremy Jones.

Architecture has always had an influence on metalsmithing. This was acknowledged in a 1988 MAG Ontario show entitled *Spatial Inclinations: Architectural Influences*. The jury wrote that it was "refreshed" in looking at the body of work submitted. There were post-modern pieces by Jackie Anderson, with her *Facade #1* pin and stand, and Kye-yeon Son, who took best-in-show (see Fig. 62). There were also more personal architectural influences in Andrew Goss's *Roof Pins* (Fig. 63), which were miniatures of houses he had known, and in Tracy Bright's set of pins, depicting a house on a hill, in a field, on the prairie, and in the dark (Plate 30). Bright's flat, graphic approach depicted the houses in isolated geographic settings. All of these pieces hinted that Canadian jewellery need only examine its own house for inspiration.

That was precisely the point of a 1989 exhibition entitled *Personal Geography: Interior Mythology.* David Rice, of Winnipeg, won best-in-show for a neckpiece entitled *Fetish* (Fig. 64). Julie Hartman's entry, *Shelter,* was an angular patinated container with applied windows (Plate 31). Kimberly MacHardy-Mitman's brooch *Personal Paradigm #9* outlined a central crossing, between edges of sterling, ebony, pearl, copper and red African wood.

Richard Finney, of Winnipeg, turned to jewellery after receiving a fine arts degree from the University of Manitoba. Finney found inspiration in religious architecture and the prairie landscape. His *Church Bracelet* (Fig. 65) is a 15-centimetre-high sterling silver sculpture of a lonely stone church.

In 1988, the Olympic Arts Festival for the Calgary Olympic Games organized *Restless Legacies: Contemporary Craft Practice in Canada.* The exhibition catalogue included essays by Tony Bloom and Lorne Falk. Bloom found the vision of craft to be maturing. He emphasized that craft was "rooted in a rich tradition of utility," but that it was also "asserting its right to be regarded as art." He regarded the fact that craft was a growth industry as proof of its cultural relevance. In his essay, Lorne Falk, a curator and contemporary art critic, discussed the social place of craft in contemporary life. He noted craft's attention to post-industrial society and to the "production of meaning."

The four metalsmiths represented in the exhibition were experimenting with legacies. Jackie Anderson's pin and stand, entitled *Show Home* (Plate 32), was a set piece of postmodern forms created from both traditional materials (sterling silver, gold and sugilite) and twentieth-century products (acrylic, polyester resin and mylar). In Fay Rooke's fine enamel piece *Passage No. 108,* she pushed past the limits of traditional enamelling. The pierced copper base and freely formed metal perfectly fit the abstraction of the enamel. Kye-yeon Son's approach was more formal. In *Deviating Lines,* she broke away from the traditional bowl format. Using married-metal techniques, she rimmed

Fig. 63. Andrew Goss   Roof Pin #1, Roof Pin #2, 1988, patinated brass, aluminum, paint. Photo: Jeremy Jones.

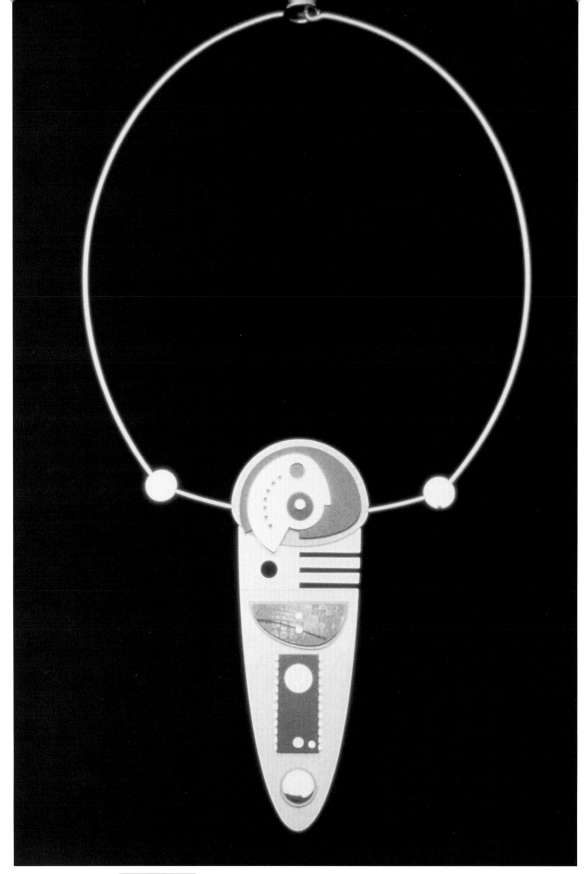

Fig. 64. | D a v i d   R i c e | Fetish (neckpiece), 1989, nickel and sterling silver, copper, gold, solicor, 5 x 12.5 cm. Photo: Jeremy Jones.

Plate 1. | Hero Kielman | renderings for rings, c. 1960.

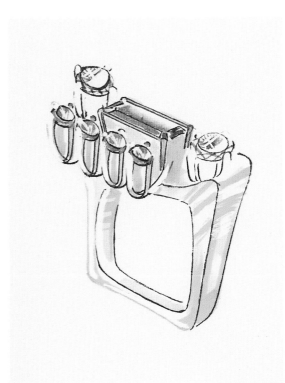

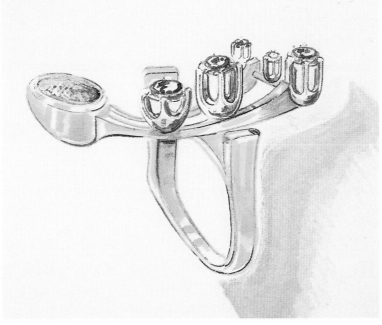

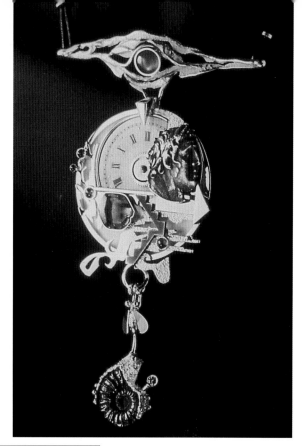

Plate 2. | Karl Heinz Stittgen | Harmoni Mundi (pendant), 1984, 18-karat gold, silver, steel, star sapphire, emeralds, watermelon tourmaline, diamond, ammonite. Photo: Peter Hogan.

Plate 3. | Ludwig Nickel | ring (top), 1987, enamel, 18-karat gold; box (bottom), 1987, enamel, 18-karat gold.

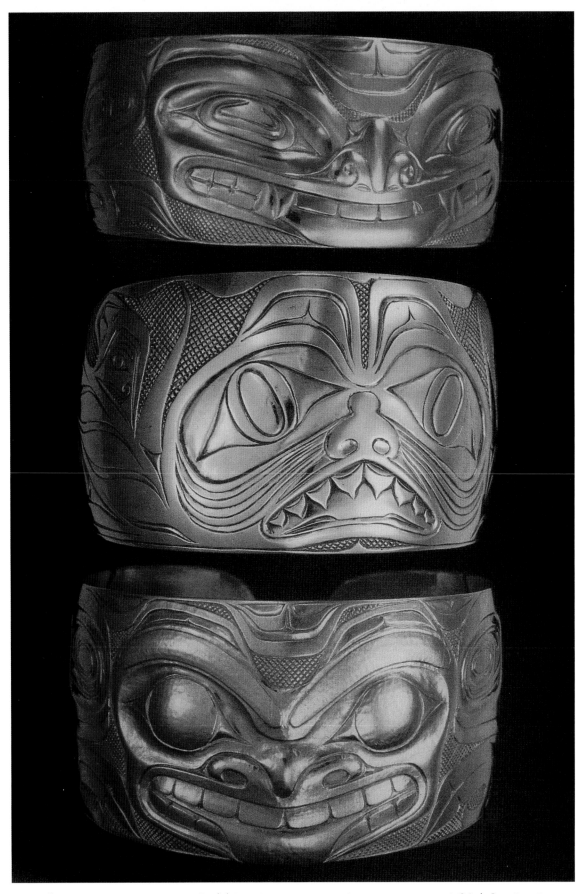

Plate 4. Bill Reid bracelets: Wolf (top), 1962, gold (gift of W. C. Koerner); Dogfish (middle), c. 1961, sterling silver (gift of Bessie Fitzgerald estate); Grizzly Bear (bottom), c. 1958, gold (gift of Bessie Fitzgerald estate). Collection: Museum of Anthropology, University of British Columbia. Photo: Bill McLennan.

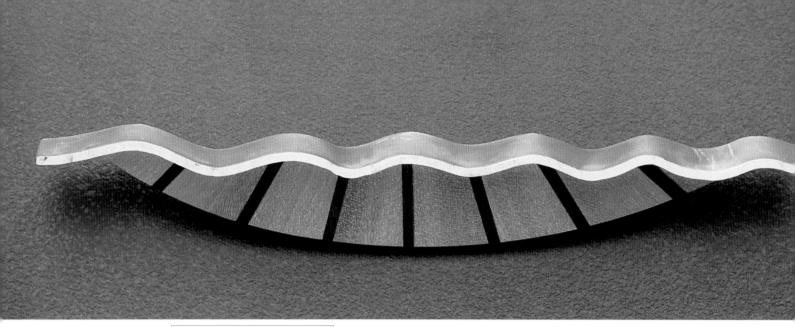

Plate 5.　Paula and Michael Letki　brooch, 1991, sterling silver, kingwood, satinwood, 7.5 x 2.5 x 1 cm.

Plate 6.　David Swinson　Tuna/Thon, 1985, sterling silver, paint, 8.5 cm in diameter.

Plate 7. | Pamela Ritchie | brooch, from The Twelve Children of Niobe, 1982, niobium, sterling silver, pearl.

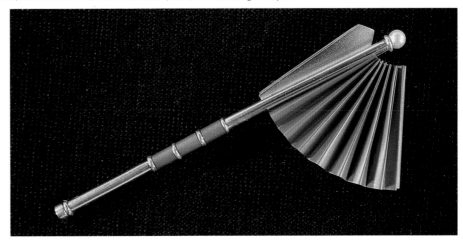

Plate 8. | David McAleese and Alison Wiggins | brooch, 1989, titanium, sterling silver, anodized, constructed, 11 x 1.2 cm. Photo: Jeremy Jones.

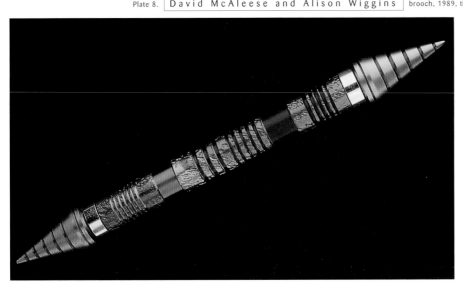

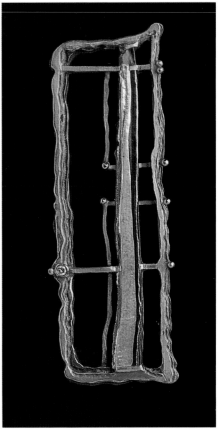

Plate 9. | Neil Carrick Aird | Sawform (brooch), 1982, yellow and white gold, sterling silver, nickel, aluminum, niobium, diamond, 5 x 7 cm. Photo: Ed Gatner.

Plate 10. Lois E. Betteridge | Ice-Cream Cone, 1983, sterling silver, vermeil and pearl, photographs, 10 x 7 cm. Photo: Keith Betteridge.

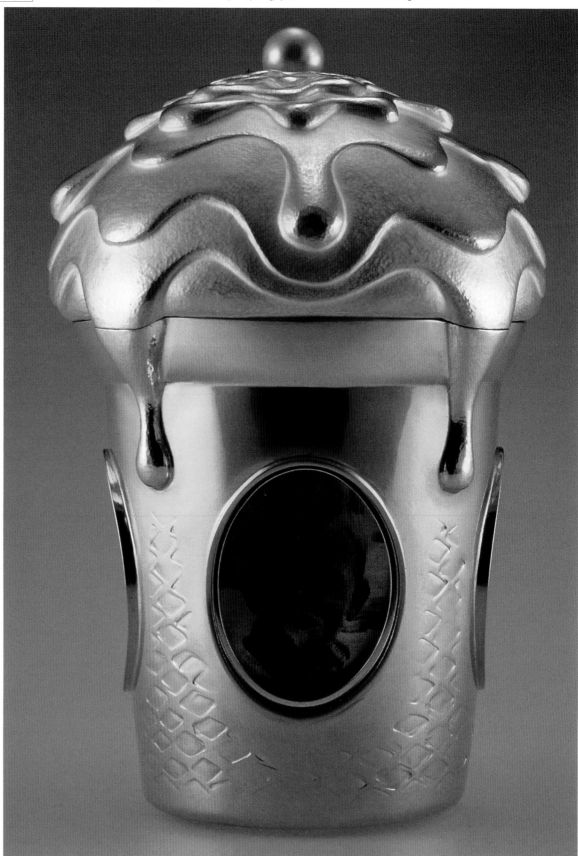

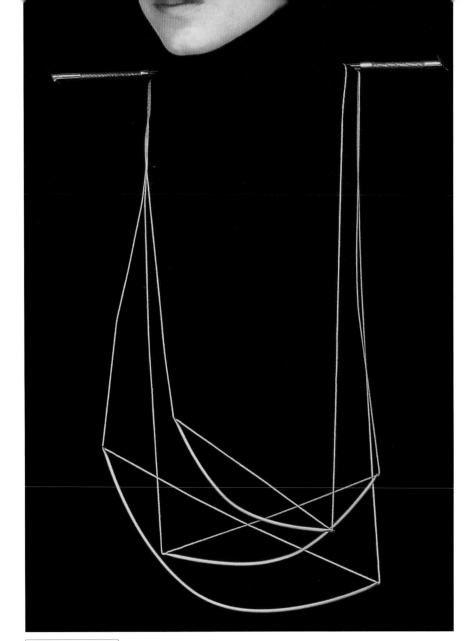

Plate 12. Betty Walton Wearable Wall-hanging, 1986, aluminum, string, acrylic, sterling silver, anodized, fabricated, 44 cm in length.

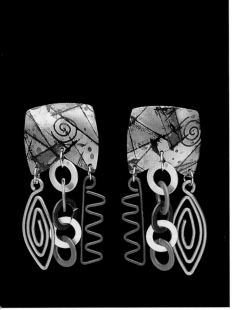

Plate 11. Diane Hanson earrings, 1995, aluminum, anodized, fabricated. Photo: Jeremy Jones.

Plate 13. | Richard Karpyshin | Party Jewellery (two of a series of brooches on photographs), 1983, enamel on copper, steel, fabricated, 5 x 7.5 cm. (brooches).

Plate 15. Paul Leathers brooch, 1987, sterling silver, light stick (cyalume rod), fabricated, 6.5 x 7 cm.

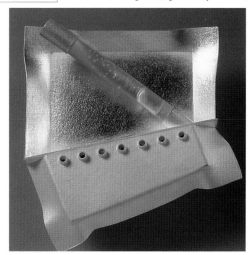

Plate 14. David Didur Medal for Dishonour (neckpiece), 1983, firecrackers, industrial iron pendant, matches, fuse.

Plate 16. Martha Glenny   Entry Charm (bracelet), 1987, cancelled tickets, sterling silver, laminated, fabricated, 17.5 cm. in diameter.

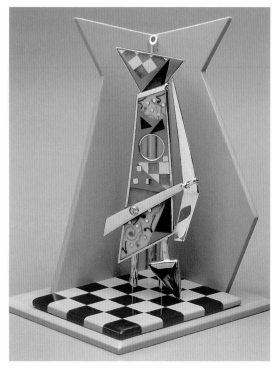

Plate 17. Jackie Anderson   Eamons (pin and stand), 1986, sterling silver, diamond, amethyst, acrylic, polyester resin, 9 x 8.7 x 8.7 cm. Collection: Illingworth Kerr Gallery, Calgary.

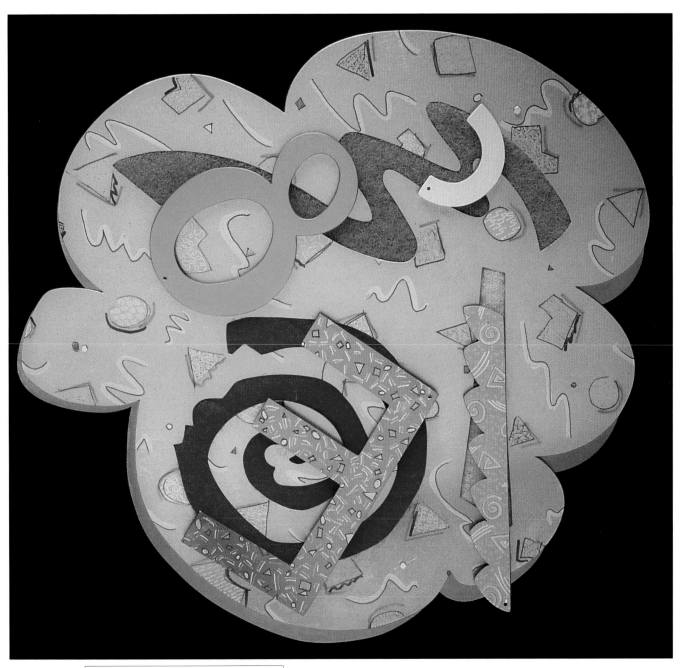

Plate 18. | D i a n e   H a n s o n   a n d   O k s a n a   K i t | wallpiece with removable shapes, 1986, anodized aluminum, Velcro, fabricated, 26 x 26 cm. Photo: Jeremy Jones.

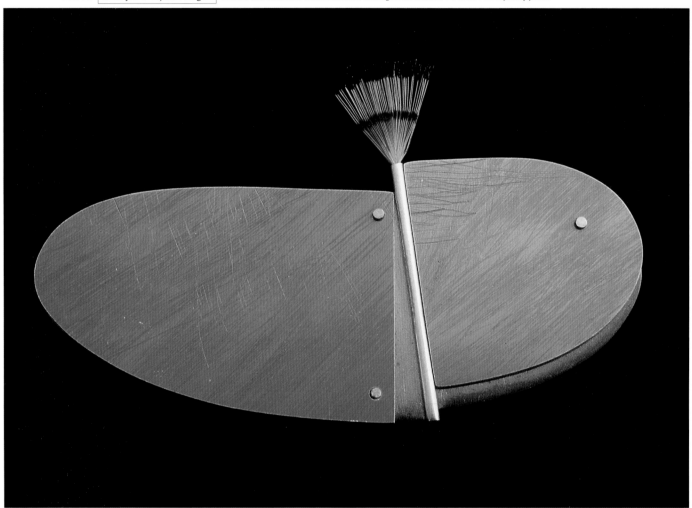

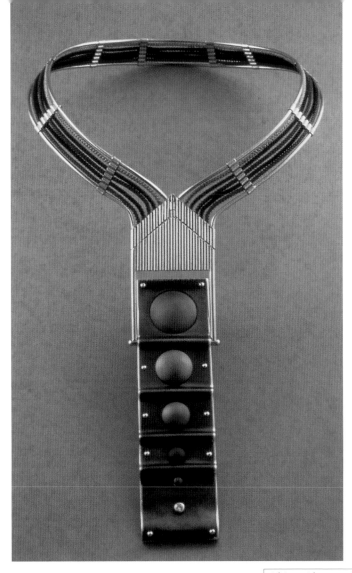

Plate 20. | A k i r a I k e g a m i | neckpiece, 1983, 18-karat yellow gold, sterling silver, niobium, shakudo, diamond, 16 x 14 cm.

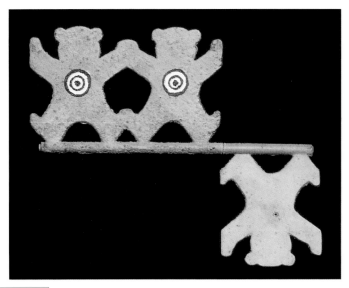

Plate 21. | B r o o k e B a i l l i e | brooch, 1987, brass, paint, fabricated, patinated, 7.1 x 2.9 cm. Photo: Jeremy Jones.

Plate 22. B r e n d a B e a r E p p three scarab pins on stand, 1988, patinated copper, moose hair, walnut stand with steel and bronze legs, gold foil, 50 cm. high. Collection: Royal Ontario Museum, Toronto. Photo: Ed Gatner.

Plate 23. **Anne Barros** Kool-Aid Container, 1988, tin-plated steel, paint, fabricated, 30 cm. Photo: Jeremy Jones.

Plate 24. David Didur New Moon in Rimouski, 1988, copper, 33 cm. high. Photo: Jeremy Jones.

Plate 25. | Fay Rooke | Autumn Garden Passage, 1984, fine silver cloisonné enamel on raised, pierced copper base; fine silver paillons, high-fire surface, 21 x 16 x 4 cm.

Plate 26. | Alan Perkins | Massey Hall 1894 (drawing), 1984–85, enamel on copper, graphite, 45 x 60 cm.

Plate 27. ☐ J a m e s D o r a n ☐ Check Mate, 1989, enamel, copper, 35 x 35 x 7.5 cm.

Plate 28. Kai Chan bodypiece, 1984, palm leaves, acrylic paint, silk, cotton, 51 x 41 x 8 cm. Photo: Peter Hogan.

Plate 29. Louis Tortell bracelet, 1984, stainless steel, aluminum, alloys of copper, silver and gold, silk, fabricated, 12 x 3.5 cm. Photo: Peter Hogan.

Plate 30. ⌈ T r a c y   B r i g h t ⌉ set of four pins (House on a Hill, House in a Field, House on the Prairie, House in the Dark), 1988, patinated brass. Photo: Jeremy Jones.

Plate 31. │ J u l i e   H a r t m a n │ Shelter (container), 1989, brass, constructed, patinated, 11.5 x 5 cm. Photo: Jeremy Jones.

Plate 32. │ J a c k i e   A n d e r s o n │ Show Home (pin and stand), 1986, sterling silver, sugilite, 14-karat gold, acrylic polyester resin, 7.2 x 10 x 5.2 cm.

Plate 33. | Lyn Wiggins | Triplet (earrings), 1992, sterling silver, 14-karat yellow gold, iolite, sugilite, fabricated, fused, 8 x 4 cm. Photo: Jeremy Jones.

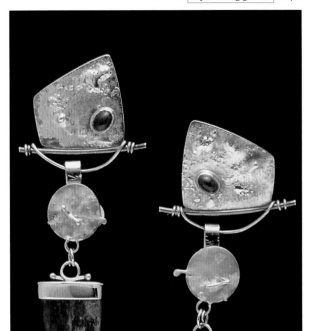

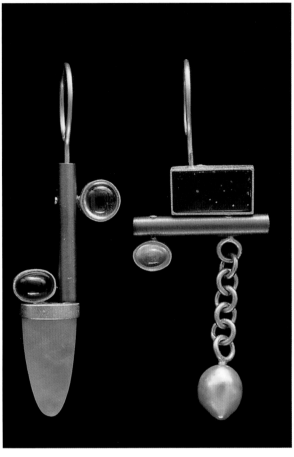

Plate 34. | Janis Kerman | earrings, 1991, 18-karat gold, tantalum, sterling silver, lapis lazuli, pearl, citrine, aquamarine, rose quartz, moonstone, fabricated 2 x 5 cm. each. Photo: Jeremy Jones.

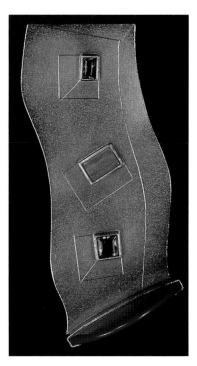

Plate 35. [Shelley Matthews-Blair] brooch, 1991, 18-karat yellow gold, sterling silver, jasper wedge, citrine, opal, peridot, fabricated, oxidized, 5 x 9 cm.

Plate 36. [Charles Lewton-Brain] Glasses, 1988, sterling silver, 24-karat gold, steel mesh, peep holes, brass, fabricated, 15 x 7.5 cm.

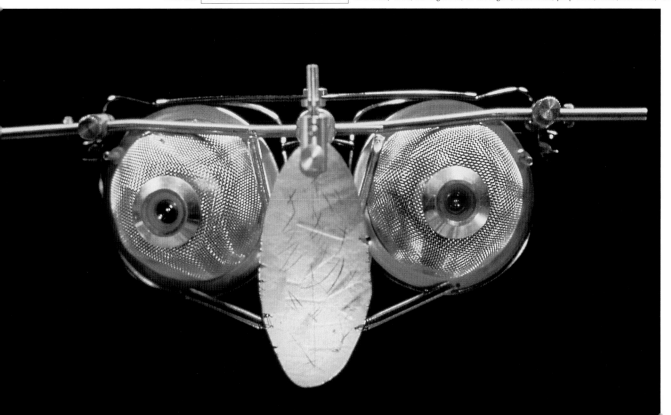

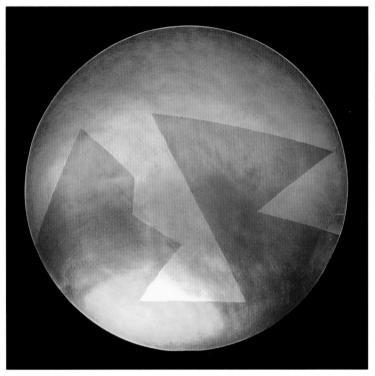

Plate 37. | D. Marie Jardine | Marriage Bowl, 1992, copper and brass, married metals, raised, 10 cm. in diameter.

Plate 38. | Mel Wolski | Hockey Game #2 (detail), 1991, brass, copper, sterling silver, steel, rubber, ceramic base (by Greg Sloane), constructed, married metals, 55 x 41.8 cm.

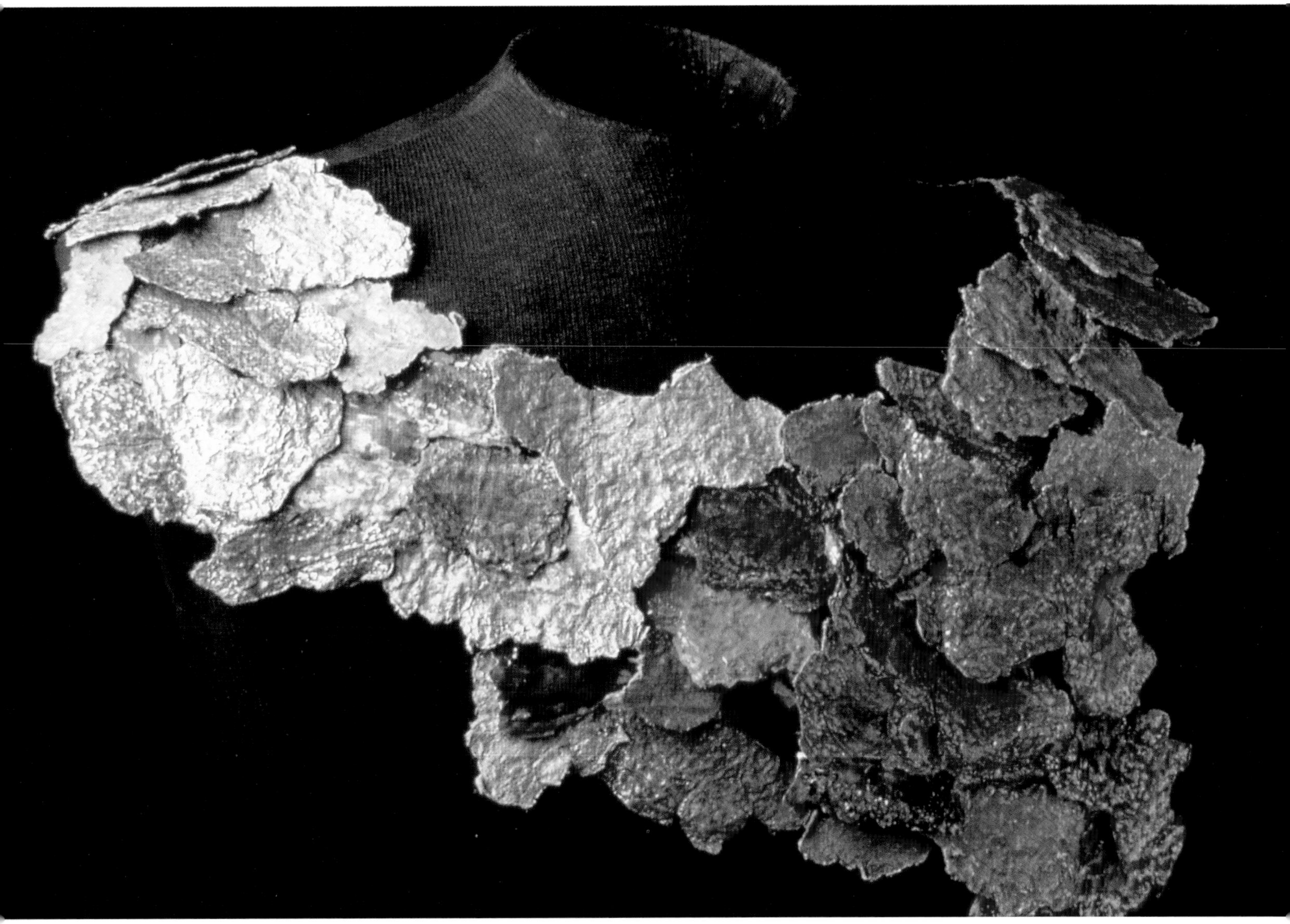

Plate 39. Madeleine Dansereau Artemis (neckpiece), 1987, handmade paper.

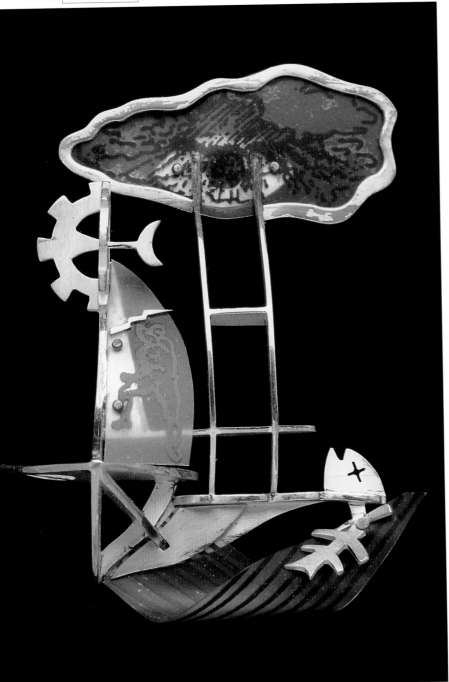

Plate 42. | Susan Wakefield | bracelet from series How My Garden Grows, 1994, sterling silver, brass, copper, tourmaline, garnet, turquoise, moonstone, peridot, amethyst, fabricated, patinated. Photo: Ed Gatner.

Plate 43. | Doreen Lapointe | Pick a Pepper, 1994, bronze with patinas, 15 x 3 cm., 10 x 2 cm., 5 x 3.5 cm.

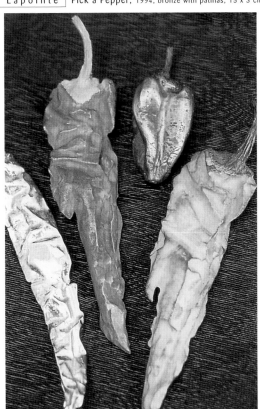

Plate 44. │ J o s é e   D e s j a r d i n s │ Eruca Sativa (brooch), 1994, sterling silver, enamel, pebble, cast, 2.5 x 6 cm.

Plate 45. │ J o s é e   D e s j a r d i n s │ Nais Vulgare (brooch), 1994, sterling silver, 18-karat gold, enamel, pebble, lost-wax casting, 1.5 x 6 cm.

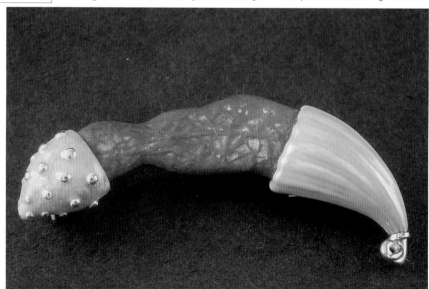

Plate 46. **Anne Fauteux** Rouages de la Pensée (set of three rings), 1994, sterling silver, bronze, brass, turquoise, acrylic.

Plate 47. **Anne Fauteux** Détourneur de Doutes (ring), 1992, sterling silver, copper, carnelian, doorbell, constructed, patinated, 40 x 25 x 20 mm.

Plate 48. | Michel-Alain Forgues | sculpture, 1991, sterling silver, copper, niobium.

Plate 49. Barbara Stutman   Raped (neckpiece), 1993, fine and sterling silver, copper, brass, magnet wire, cotton, spool knitting, crochet, 30 x 18 cm. Photo: Pierre Fauteux.

Plate 50. Faith Layard   Arc to Woods (brooch), 1992, fine silver, copper, enamel, cloisonné, fabricated, 5.5 x 4.5 cm.

Plate 51. Ken Vickerson Totem (brooch), 1991, sterling silver, nickel, copper, mokume gane, diamond, laminated, fabricated, 5.7 x 5.5 x .2 cm.

Fig. 65. Richard Finney Church Bracelet, 1988, sterling silver, cast, fabricated, 15.5 x 6.5 x 7 cm.

the top of the bowl with wire. The wire returned to penetrate the bowl's side and act as a foot for the piece. Finally, Louis Tortell worked spring-like strands of aluminum with silk for a neckpiece that exploited the materials to their fullest in the interest of beauty and function.

Although Canadian society may have been unaware of these metalsmiths, in the metalsmithing community they became models of artistic achievement and furthered the feeling that something good was happening in this country. Their output embodied some of the best ideas and explorations of the eighties.

New Galleries

The booming eighties economy had its impact on Canadian jewellery sales, and new galleries featuring fine craft opened in great numbers. There was Fireworks Gallery, in Halifax; Gallery Suk Kwan, in Montreal; Gallery Lynda Greenberg, in Ottawa; Metalworks, in Kingston;

Harbinger Gallery, in Waterloo; Metal + David Rice Studios, in Winnipeg; Electrum Design Studio, in Edmonton; and Provenance, in Calgary. In Toronto, Prime Canadian Crafts, Bounty at Harbourfront, the Guild Shop, In the Making, Dexterity, the Kensington Silver Studio and Harhay & MacKay, among others, vied for the public's attention. And in Vancouver, the Cartwright Street Gallery competed with other small galleries on Granville Island. In most provinces, craft councils sold jewellery and metal art in their craft shops, and innumerable other small craft stores sold handmade pieces.

The first Canadian gallery to devote itself totally to art jewellery, however, was that of Jocelyne Gobeil, in Montreal. According to an article by Enid Kaplan, in *Metalsmith*, Gobeil chose Montreal because she considered it the "most European of large North American cities," and because Montrealers are "unconventional and daring." Initially, Gobeil's goal was to represent only Quebec jewellery artists, but after two years she began showing the work of an international group of artists, many of whom were defining the history of twentieth-century jewellery. From the beginning, in its exhibition and sale, she approached jewellery as art. One of her most important achievements was the acceptance of her gallery by the Contemporary Art Gallery Association. Like Suzann Greenaway at Prime Gallery, in an effort to educate the public, Gobeil promoted art jewellery through lectures and exhibitions of avant-garde and conceptual work.

This burgeoning of fine craft galleries and exhibitions marked a distinct change from previous decades. In the past, the winning entries of a show would be photographed together against a textile backdrop. But now, professional photographers were being hired to document each piece individually. Before 1986, members of MAG Ontario would send only their best pieces to the annual show. But by the late eighties, most shows challenged participants with a theme. As craft galleries began to behave more like art galleries, it became more difficult to book shows of disparate metalwork.

The eighties marked the apex of the explosion in jewellery and hollowware after the Second World War. The exploration of techniques and new materials, the diversity in forms and fastenings, the shift from formal design to personal expression, and, finally, the many exhibition and sales opportunities provided by a period of economic boom, made for this culmination of twenty years of quiet working.

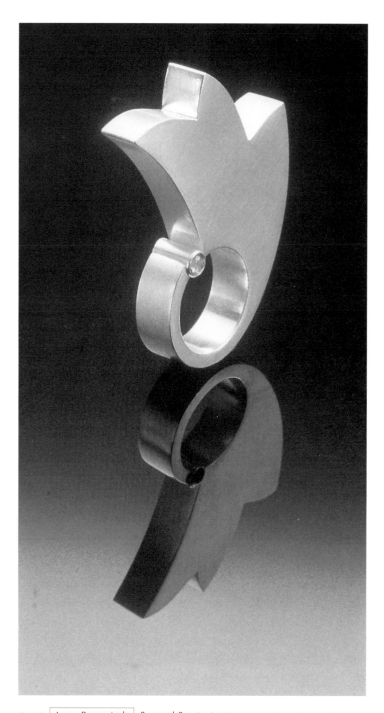

82

Fig. 66. │ J o y   P e n n i c k │ Sun and Sea (ring), 1991, sterling silver, 24-karat gold, synthetic stone, fabricated, keum-boo, 4 x 5 x 1 cm. Photo: George Georgakakos.

The 1990s:

Postmodern Metal

Metalcraft as Art

Faith Popcorn, a renowned market forecaster, predicted that the nineties would be a period of cocooning. Unfortunately, a worldwide recession in the early nineties left the cocooner with no disposable income and often no job. Because jewellery is a luxury, sales plummeted. Major jewellery store chains went into bankruptcy, and studio jewellers suffered dramatic losses of income. Along with the recession, the political climate of cutbacks and deficit reduction hit the arts hard.

To sell jewellery as art is not easy, since art is usually perceived as something to hang on the wall, not the body. Although the jewellery of ancient Egypt and Greece has found a place in art-history textbooks, contemporary art jewellery gets very little attention. In an article in *Metalsmith,* Enid Kaplan quotes German critic Reinhold Ludwig as saying that "nearly all of the superior quality artistic jewelry available is grossly undervalued when compared with graphics, photography, paintings and sculptures." According to Toronto jeweller Peter Cullman, the public at large does not understand that unique handmade jewellery is art. Art jewellers are anxious to have their work exhibited as art. But for jewellery to compete in the art market it must be able to withstand the scrutiny of the art critic. Metalsmiths need to base their craft on coherent theories that can be articulated and appreciated by a consumer society. The fact that contemporary glass and ceramics have found some success with collectors and museums is often looked to as encouragement that metal art will follow suit.

Jocelyne Gobeil believes that some jewellery will finally be accepted within the category of fine arts. With a growing number of fine-craft galleries in North America, the rigid separation of art and craft — of fineness and function — is falling away. For years craft has borrowed the terminology of art; so much so that few public viewers at metal-art exhibits are as familiar with the terms *planished, reticulated,* and *keum-boo,* as they are with *colour field, impasto* and *gesso.* Because the idea of jewellery as art is still quite young, little criticism, and even less written history, exist. Some believe that metalcraft will not be fully accepted as art until there is a critical base of scholarship that cannot be ignored. Yet others see no need to adopt a "craftspeak" after they have witnessed the obfuscation of artspeak. The world of craft, according to art critic Robert Hughes, currently contributes fresh ideas to the world of art.

Marketing

Hoping to learn new strategies, nineties jewellers flocked to workshops and conferences on marketing. They wanted to make a living from their work, but needed to learn how to wholesale, how to get their work into galleries, how to find sales representatives, and how to package their work.

A range of marketing options, from one-of-a-kind commission work to wholesale production, was studied intently. At a 1995 conference entitled *To Market, to Market,* Suzann Greenaway, of Prime Gallery, remarked that when she sold craft-based art she was not as much looking for a market as she was trying to find a "mate" for a piece. Some jewellers chose to supplement their art jewellery with production lines of less expensive jewellery. In the past, such production work had been scorned by art jewellers, who usually could not abide its repetition, and by gallery owners, who wanted one-of-a-kind pieces. But by the late eighties there was a change in attitude, and in the nineties, well-designed production work was being marketed that demanded attention.

Sandra Noble Goss and Andrew Goss, of Owen Sound, Ontario, have consistently displayed excellence in design and technique in their reasonably priced production work, which they sell across Canada. Vivienne Jones and Lyn Wiggins, also from Ontario, are also respected for their fine limited-production jewellery. Along with one-of-a-kind pieces like *Triplet* (Plate 33), which demand her goldsmithing skills, Wiggins has experimented with electrical discharge machining (EDM). Through this method, she reproduced Canadian artist Michael Snow's iconic image of *The Walking Woman,* in limited editions, for the Art Gallery of Ontario.

In Newfoundland, Debra Kuzyk produces silk-screened earrings and brooches in rich colours for a local market. Joy Pennick, of Nova Scotia, founder of *Joy Jewellery and Metalworks,* expanded her wholesale market through the Atlantic Craft Trade Shows. Her simple, organic forms, often die-formed, express her interest in nature. *Sun and Sea* (Fig. 66), for example, is a hollow, constructed sterling silver ring that represents a common Nova Scotia phenomenon — the sun rising over the crest of a wave. Mimi Shulman's distinctive *Tokens of Gilt* line features cast pieces warmly adorned with hearts and flowers. The brooch *Waiting* (Fig. 67) is a romantic portrayal of a woman who has just let her book fall back on the pillow. Despite the effusiveness of the scene, the woman's serious demeanour compounds the work's complexity.

Janis Kerman, of Montreal, who had designed a less expensive line of jewellery, often using colour core, has since shifted her interest toward coloured stones and precious metals. Her earrings (Plate 34) do not match, but complement each other with just the right formal placement of stones, pearl, chain and tubular elements.

Shelley Matthews-Blair, also of Montreal, uses long silver forms as palettes for stones that she sells to galleries across Canada. On the brooch shown in Plate 35, she added geometric engraving on the oxidized surface to create changing perspectives for the stones.

At the more expensive end of the scale, OCA graduate Beni Sung was a model of success. Sung designed elegant jewellery, which was often fabricated outside of Canada. He became a success in his early thirties, with an international clientele and his own boutique in downtown Toronto. Fashion and society pages revelled in Sung's work, but beneath the glamour was a hard-working and serious artist. He is best remembered for his use of large freshwater pearls, which he relished for their individuality and subtlety. Sung won many awards. His diamond-and-onyx collar (Fig. 68), made for the 1984 Diamonds International competition, was a hinged masterpiece that perfectly fit the contours of the neck. The hinges were concealed behind rows of diamonds.

The greatest Canadian success story in the marketing of metalwork has been in pewter. John Caraberis and Bonnie Ward began Seagull Pewter and Silversmiths, in Pugwash, Nova Scotia, in 1978. Today it is a multi-million-dollar business that employs the latest production equipment for cast and spun wares. The firm has been a good employer for local people and a boon to the provincial craft economy. New Brunswick also boasts an enviable pewter community, which was begun by Dr. Ivan Crowell and carried on by Aitkens Pewter, Carole Cronkhite, and many others.

Bernard Chaudron and Paul Simard, in Val-David, Quebec, and Greg and Suzanne Amos, in Mahone Bay, Nova Scotia, have found that pewter offers greater artistic flexibility and financial opportunity than other metals. Pewter has long been appreciated for its low cost and relative ease in forming. Lois E. Betteridge is credited with bringing pewter back to public attention in the nineties with an exhibition entitled *Pewterworkings,* which included over a hundred pieces from across the country. Coinciding with the release of the book *For the Love of Pewter: Pewterers of Canada,* by Douglas Shenstone, the show not only

Fig. 67. | Mimi Shulman | Waiting (brooch), 1987, sterling silver, 14-karat yellow gold, antique ceramic button, cast, 15 x 9 cm.

Fig. 68. | Beni Sung | collar, 1984, onyx, diamonds, fabricated, hinged. Winner in DeBeers International competition. Photo: Diamond Information Centre, Toronto.

Fig. 69. | Pamela Ritchie | vase, 1990, pewter, fabricated, 12.7 x 21 x 3.5 cm. Photo: George Georgakakos.

presented the work of noted pewtersmiths but challenged other met-alsmiths to work in the soft metal. Catherine Windust, of Waterloo, Ontario, stressed the metal's easy fluidity in a salt-and-pepper set; Antoine Lamarche, of Montreal, a jeweller who usually works in gold and silver, raised a large container with patinated brass exterior and pewter interior; Pamela Ritchie, of Halifax, created a flower vase in a flower shape (Fig. 69); and Shayne Kjertinge, a graduate of OCA, cre-ated a series of six brooches, entitled *Inner Series*. Kjertinge's brooches were intricately focussed, like small paintings, and explored

shape and line in an abstract yet emotional manner. Kjertinge layered and riveted the metals to draw the viewer into a complex inner world.

Marketing of the arts was a hot topic in the early nineties. The federal government commissioned Price-Waterhouse to study the visual arts and crafts. It found that public awareness and market development were among the pivotal challenges to development in the art and craft sectors. This was no news to craftspeople or to some provincial governments. The government of Saskatchewan and the Saskatchewan Craft Council already recognized craft as a cultural industry. Other provinces provided useful information and encouraged the export of Canadian craft, especially to U.S. border states. The Nova Scotia Designer Crafts Council managed the Atlantic Craft Trade Shows — important sales venues for the east coast.

In Quebec, marketing has been promoted by the Conseil des métiers d'art du Québec, which is the only official association for craftspersons working professionally in the province. From its two galleries, a seventeen-day exhibition held each December in Montreal, and the ten-day Festival Plein Art Québec, held each August in Quebec City, the Conseil generates annual sales of eight million dollars. It also stages a prestigious biennial that travels in Canada and other countries. Quebec, more than any of the provinces, recognizes craft and art as important parts of its cultural policy. The ledger shows that craft as a cultural industry can be a good business investment.

Quebec jewellers have also benefited from the patronage of their provincial government in the yearly Prix du Québec, which honours literary and scientific achievement with monetary awards and medals designed and made by Quebec metalsmiths. In 1992, for example, Bruno Gérard was chosen to create the medal for the Prix Léon-Gérin (Fig. 70).

Some artists participate in studio tours, in which they join with other local artists in sending out invitations and then open their doors to travelling patrons. In many parts of the country, colourful maps of artists' studio locations are printed, and the public roam the countryside in search of crafts.

With jewellery sales down, some artists have shifted their attention to eyeglasses as jewellery. Charles Lewton-Brain and Dee Fontans, both of Calgary, and Mila Rolicz, of Toronto, exhibited wacky eyewear in a large show in Portland, Oregon, in 1994. Lewton-Brain's *Glasses I* (Plate 36) are made of steel mesh and door peep holes, with a brass leaf hanging down as a nose shade. Their mocking humour played with ideas of security and identity, and poked fun at the designer eyeware industry.

The shifting of the nineties market from jewellery to objects has given hollowware a boost. Most hollowware is now in non-precious metals, and has a postmodern feel. Peter Currie, of Toronto, designed a series of vessels and stands using tantalum, steel and wood. The incorporation of these colourful finishes into hollowware continues the colour impetus in what used to be a fairly monochromatic discipline. As if to remind us of the clear forms of modernism, Jemmy Fung, a graduate of OCA, produced a neo-modernist steel fruit tray (Fig. 71). The tray rocks on a sleek, arcing base. A guardrail of fine steel wire

87

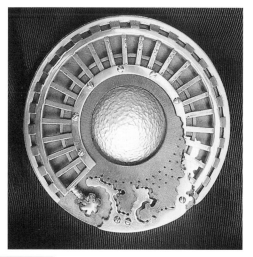

Fig. 70. | B r u n o   G é r a r d | medal for the Prix Léon-Gérin, 1992.

Fig. 71. | J e m m y   F u n g | fruit tray, 1991, nickel steel, stainless-steel wire, 45 x 11 x 8.5 cm.

holds the fruit in place and insures function with sculptural form. The hollowware of D. Marie Jardine, a graduate of NSCAD, relies on married metals for its colour and strong graphic images. Her aptly titled *Marriage Bowl* (Plate 37) underlines the technique of working two different metals as one, with positive and negative vying for dominance. Mel Wolski, a technician at Georgian College, in Barrie, Ontario, also works with married metals. He expresses his love for Canada's leading sport in *Hockey Game #2* (Plate 38), in which skaters made of copper and brass scurry for the puck.

As an entrepreneurial way of celebrating their history, three Montreal jewellers, Claudette Hardy-Pilon, Jean-Eudes Germain and Michel Larbrisseau, create small bronze busts of historical figures. Jacques Cartier and Madeleine de Verchères come to life, with expressive eyes and finely worked hair and clothing. But earning a livelihood in the nineties, these jewellers agree, leaves little time for research or exploration of ideas.

Most public art galleries across Canada sell Canadian-made jewellery in their gift shops, which are usually run by volunteer committees. In 1994, the Montreal Museum of Fine Arts took an additional step by inviting jewellery artists to use its museum collection for inspiration. This resulted in many startlingly good new works, and both the museum and the artists benefited from the collaboration.

Commissioned pieces are often the most process-oriented work, involving lengthy sessions to discover the client's wishes, draw sketches, and collaborate on design, but it is very rewarding for many artists. The nineties have seen a renewed interest in commissioned jewellery and hollowware. Endless self-expression is very demanding, and turning to another's needs and habits can be a valued respite. Seeing one's work displayed in someone's home can also be more satisfying to the artist than seeing it in the sterility of the gallery.

Beginning with gold buttons affixed to a long beaver coat presented to Queen Victoria, Canada's ties to Britain have resulted in many important commissions for Canadian metalsmiths. But commissions come from many sources. In 1993, the Task Force on Gender Equality in the Legal Profession asked Sarabeth Carnat to design a brooch in honour of Supreme Court Justice Bertha Wilson. The Canadian Bar Association then sold variations of the pin to its members as a fundraiser to help implement the recommendations of the task force. Carnat's brooch portrayed the symbols for gender and justice within the classical portals of a court entrance, and visually captured the social and legal debate.

After eight years of concentrating on jewellery exhibitions and sales in her gallery, Jocelyne Gobeil said that she was disappointed with most Canadian jewellers. According to Gobeil, she had found "very few Canadian jewellers with good technical skills, a clear personal vision and a strong desire to really question themselves and make better work." The incredible demands of creating high-quality work for a very narrow audience and earning one's livelihood from that work is met by only a few art jewellers in Canada. Most must make compromises, either in their work or in their lifestyle.

The most difficult thing for most metalsmiths to accept is compromise in design. In much production jewellery of the nineties there is a similarity that suggests a cloning of shapes, surface textures and images. Similarly, the so-called "urban primitive" trend that espoused a rough approach to metal was often a facade for careless technique. The decline of experimentation in favour of safe production is a response not only to the marketplace but to the lack of critical dialogue in Canadian crafts in general. Favourable reviews are now the norm. Critical evaluations of exhibition pieces could demand a more thoughtful approach to design.

Education

Many of the college-level metal programs were as volatile as the stock market during the eighties and nineties. In 1984, Humber College's Metal Arts program, set up by Hero Kielman in 1975, was axed by an administration that cared more about employment numbers than about the cultural life of the community. The well-equipped studios were torn out and converted to classrooms for teaching aspiring travel agents — a much cheaper way of filling employment quotas. In 1986, the metal and weaving studios that had begun with Sheridan College's School of Crafts and Design, in 1967, were closed.

The Jewellery and Metals program at Georgian College, on the other hand, was carefully developed over a period of years. It went from a conventional metal-art curriculum to a unique cooperative education approach. While learning bench and design skills, the Georgian student now spends set periods working in the jewellery industry at some level. As its director and founder, Don Stuart has been able to use not only his silversmithing and design abilities but also his influence in the metal community. As a member of the SNAG board of directors and as past president of the Ontario Crafts Council, he has been able to launch a program that could be used as a model for others in Canada.

Another educational success is Sturgeon Creek Collegiate, in Winnipeg, which offers a jewellery arts certificate and boasts that seventy percent of its graduates have found employment in the jewellery trade. Headed by Alan Doherty, a graduate of NSCAD, the program appeals to students looking for vocational training as well as to craftspeople wanting to learn a new skill.

But Canada's largest jewellery program remains at George Brown College, in Toronto. George Brown attracts hundreds of applicants from across the country. Under the leadership of Akira Ikegami, and later, James Robson, the program has developed since the 1980s so that it now teaches both the commercial and the artistic aspects of the jewellery trade. Recent graduate shows have sought out a wider public by presenting in downtown galleries.

At OCA, under the direction of Beth Alber, the metal program, which had been an elective for forty years, became a major in 1988. As part of the Technological Studies program, an emphasis is placed on drawing skills, and a wide range of design courses is offered. The fourth year of the program is designed by the individual student and includes research, writing and making, so that the graduate ends up with a cohesive body of work and a sense of direction.

Pamela Ritchie assumed the chair of the jewellery department at NSCAD in 1985 and continued the combination of high technical standards and individuality of expression that have been key to the department's success. Ritchie, who has stressed the communicative role of jewellery, helps students to develop creative strategies and to express their ideas as best suit them individually. To allow for an intense period of study in a given area, whole courses are offered, rather than the usual two- or three-week projects. Ritchie feels that this gives the NSCAD graduate strength in a particular area rather than an overview without a specialty. With its BFA and MFA jewellery programs, the department continues to hold a preeminent reputation among schools in Canada.

Jewellery and metal programs were established in the eighties at Vancouver Community College and at the New Brunswick College of Craft and Design; and in the nineties at Arctic College in the Northwest Territories and the Kootenay School of the Arts in Nelson, British Columbia. All bring well-rounded programs to the scene. Arctic College is unique in that it strives to promote hand fabrication skills for its mostly Inuit students. This emphasis on technique prepares graduates to make and sell their own work.

Answering the need for more jewellery education in Calgary is the private school begun by Charles Lewton-Brain and Dee Fontans, both of whom hold degrees from the State University of New York at New Paltz. Among the workshop techniques offered is Lewton-Brain's innovative approach to metal forming, which he calls "fold forming." By folding and unfolding metal, either with tools or by hand, an effect is quickly achieved that resembles chased and constructed forms.

Lewton-Brain has written extensively about teaching and public relations. Among his contributions to the technical literature is his book *Cheap Thrills in the Tool Shop,* which outlines inexpensive equipment options and bench tricks for goldsmiths. But Lewton-Brain takes the important role that technical exchanges and workshops play in craft seriously. He affirms that any exploration of new methods is soon appreciated by the whole community.

In Edmonton, Karen Cantine, a graduate of the University of Iowa, uses her spacious studio to teach silversmithing to twenty-four fortunate students. The instruction is traditional in approach and very individualized. In her own work, Cantine specializes in hollowware with rounded planished forms, such as her series of *Pillow Bowls.* With curved copper bases and sunken tops, these double-walled containers suggest softness — something metal does not usually do.

Because Montreal lacked a professional jewellery school, Madeleine Dansereau and Armand Brochard founded the École de Joaillerie et de Métaux d'Art, which existed from 1972 until 1996. Along with the Saidye Bronfman Centre and the École de Joaillerie in Quebec City, it later became part of the CEGEP system. Dansereau, with fine arts degrees from the École des Beaux-Arts, Montreal, and the University of Quebec, wrote a master's thesis that outlined a new model for jewellery education in Quebec. She researched jewellery programs in other parts of the world and made recommendations for Quebec to establish a university-level program, a "Centre de formation en métiers d'art" for the small but important number of art jewellers who would unquestionably benefit from it. Dansereau saw jewellery as an art form that served the double function of ornament and communication.

Fig. 72.   Madeleine Dansereau   ICTHOS (vessel), 1990, sterling silver, gold plating, raised, fabricated.

Until her death, in 1991, Dansereau was the dynamic leader of an exciting metals scene in Montreal. Fluently bilingual in English and French, and totally dedicated to art, Dansereau devised interdisciplinary programs, invited guest artists for workshops, and, above all, stimulated others with the beauty of her own experimental work. *Artemis* (Plate 39) was one of a series of neckpieces, bibs and cuffs that evolved from her work with handmade paper. Dansereau tore the paper into fragments and then individually textured and painted each fragment. The final assemblage was a lightweight layer of shimmering colours. Her last piece, entitled *ICHTHOS* (Fig. 72), was a fish-shaped communion vessel. Its patinated exterior was engraved with a phrase from Erich Fromm: "Words are vessels that are filled with experience that overflows the vessels."

One of the most significant educational changes in the nineties has been the record number of women involved in jewellery programs both as students and faculty. Today, Beth Alber, Sarabeth Carnat, Brigitte Clavette, Enid Kaplan and Pamela Ritchie all head jewellery departments. Jewellery stores and manufacturing firms are still predominantly run by men, but many independent galleries have been established and run by women.

Aside from the training of jewellers and metal artists, schools also provide students with their first opportunities to exhibit. NSCAD, for example, has three galleries, and graduating students are required to exhibit their work as part of their course requirements. Halifax, with its many galleries, also provides the opportunity for artists to show their work. The chance to create and exhibit a body of work is important for focusing the young metalsmith's mind and hand.

The transition from the school environment, with its experimental atmosphere and tolerance for deadlines, to professional life is a difficult one. The Craft Studio at Harbourfront Centre in Toronto has

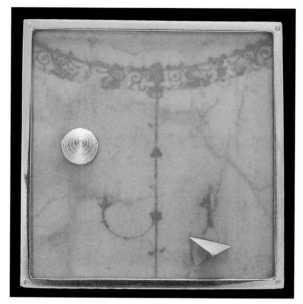

attempted to ease this transition. The program was started in 1974, when a group of recent Sheridan School of Design graduates was enlisted to take part in an experiment. They were to entertain the public through demonstrations and would each receive a hundred dollars a week. The program, held in a derelict foundry, encouraged the young metalsmiths to share their ideas and tools. From these humble beginnings this program has become an excellent opportunity for recent graduates to meet the public and exhibit their work.

Under the direction of Jean Johnson (from 1979–91) and Melanie Egan (since 1991), the studio's goals have been to promote excellence in contemporary crafts by providing education for craft professionals and the public at large. It has been a success on all counts. The visiting artist series *International Creators* has been especially stimulating for Canadian metalsmiths. The series offers lectures and workshops with foreign artists that have included Otto Künzli, Manfred Bischoff, Paul Derrez, David Watkins and Michael Rowe.

Issues and Exhibitions

While metalsmiths worried about keeping the wolf away, they also considered the issues of the day. MAG Nova Scotia chose "Water" as the theme of its 1990 show. Luc Pilon's brooch *Cause and Effects* (Plate 40) won best-in-show, with its beautiful but frightening imagery. Fabricated in sterling silver, gold and acetate, it portrayed the water cycle, with a ladder leading to an ominous cloud and a dramatic fish skeleton gasping above the waterline. Fish were well represented in the exhibition, as makers grappled with declining fish stocks and pollution.

In 1991, MAG Ontario's theme was "Resources." The show provided a forum for artists to vent their concerns about everything from the air we breathe to the conditions of our cultural resources. Ann Lumsden's brooch *In Case of Emergency* (Plate 41) took best-in-show. In Mary Pocock and Heike Raschl's brooch *Pompeii II* (Fig. 73), the artists integrated a photographic image in a sterling silver brooch, drawing attention to their concern for saving cultural monuments.

The recycling movement was another impetus for jewellers to focus on their materials. Alberta artists were challenged to use recycled materials in an exhibition in 1994 entitled *Reincarnation*. Linda Chow, a graduate of Alberta College of Art, transformed aluminum kitchenware and screening into headgear (Fig. 74). Chow felt that taking common everyday objects out of their intended context revealed their beauty.

With the rise of the environmental movement, metalsmiths began to question their own role in the inflated values of precious metals and in the environmental and societal toll that the demand for such metals has placed on the earth through mining. Though awareness has risen, there has been little action for change.

In the light of the world's environmental problems, nineties jewellers began to seek inspiration from their own garden environments. Susan Wakefield, who studied at Kent State and at the Sheridan College School of Design, designed a series of bracelets called How My Garden Grows (for an example, see Plate 42) for the 1994 Harbourfront exhibition *Beyond the Garden Wall*. Miniature garden implements, patinated leaves and coloured gemstones swung freely in her cottage garden. Van McKenzie, a graduate of George Brown College, won awards for his necklaces and bracelets, which were thick with cast sterling silver and embossed leaves (for an example, see Fig. 75). Sue Parke, of Toronto, built outdoor sculptural works. Doreen Lapointe, of Winnipeg, in her "obsession with the intricacies of nature," carved and cast bronze peppers (Plate 43).

Fig. 74. | Linda Chow | Equilibrium, 1994, aluminum deep fryer, screen, knitting needles, anodized, 58 cm. in diameter.

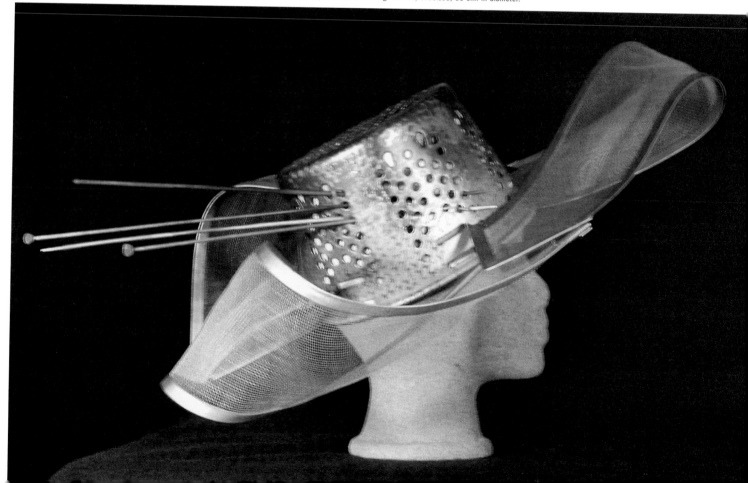

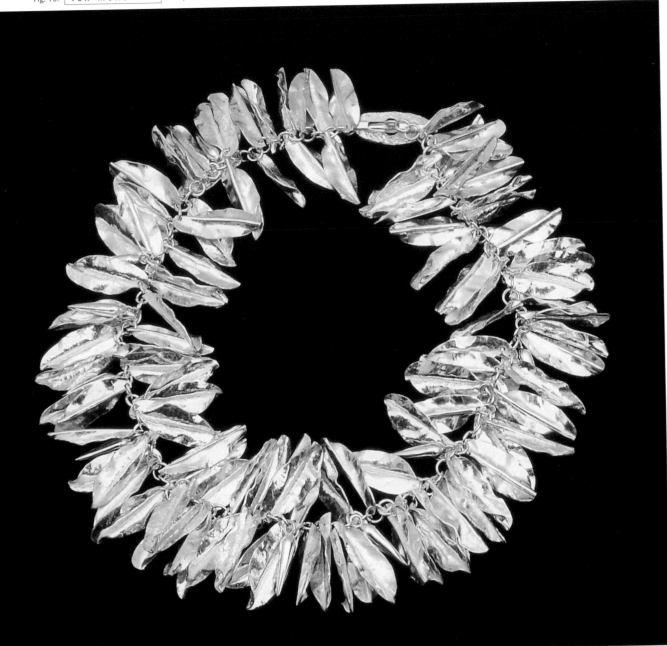

Organic forms began to replace the common geometric shapes of the eighties. Josée Desjardins, for example, a graduate of the École de Joaillerie et de Métaux d'Art de Montréal, has created a series of three-dimensional plant-like structures using metal, enamel and pebbles. In *Eruca Sativa* (Plate 44) and *Nais Vulgare* (Plate 45), her strong, vibrant colours recall Quebec's tradition in enamel. Desjardins's highly imaginative work represents the best of Canadian jewellery in the nineties.

In 1991, the Canadian Native Arts Foundation awarded Mary Anne Barkhouse — a Kwakiutl Native of British Columbia and a graduate of OCA — a grant to help her prepare for two exhibitions. Barkhouse's concept of jewellery is "not as personal adornment but as personal reference." A pair of earrings entitled *When my grandfather caught a whale in his net and had to row out to cut him loose and set him free* (Fig. 76) depicts her grandfather in a rowboat on one earring and

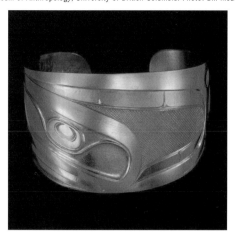

the struggling whale on the other. Wolves are another distinct theme in her work. Barkhouse cuts their silhouettes in silver to show them stretching, howling and running. A strong sense of graphic line brings her Native imagery immediately into the mainstream.

In the footsteps of Bill Reid, a number of other artists who work in metal and wood, including Haida Natives Robert Davidson, Francis Williams and Lyle Wilson, and Kwakwaka'wakw Natives Russell Smith and Lloyd Wadhams, are maintaining the West Coast Native tradition. Davidson, who has been especially innovative, views his art objects as symbols of his heritage. He believes that Native artists need to have full involvement in Native life and ceremony for their work to have integrity. His 1994 bracelet (Fig. 77) *Cormorant and Kagaan Jaad ("Mouse Woman")* shows a departure from his teacher, Bill Reid, in his use of negative space to create forms.

Of all the social and political issues facing Canadians, Quebec sovereignty has perhaps been the most contentious. Surprisingly, it has not been a predominant theme in jewellery making. One can detect differences in approach, however, between Quebec and the rest of Canada. The work of Quebec artists is in general more sculptural and three-dimensional than that usually found elsewhere. Anne Fauteux, of Montreal, believes that many jewellers, in their pursuit of artistic recognition, have adopted sculptural principles to such an extent that their work should no longer be considered jewellery. She moved from sculpture to jewellery because she found it could be "exhibited simply and at will," thus having "a direct and persistent impact on the public." In her own work, she uses enamel and found objects — such as the doorbell from her own home — for their physical and symbolic qualities (see Plates 46 + 47).

Quebec jewellery is also imbued with different passions. Where the rest of Canada seems to be forever searching for an identity, Quebec proudly embraces its French heritage. The work of Michel-Alain Forgues, with its strong forms and vibrant contrasts, draws on the sculptural past while looking to the future (for an example of his work, see Plate 48). Forgues teaches at the École de Joaillerie de Québec.

An exploration called *Cultural Baggage* (Fig. 78) was undertaken by Dominique Bréchault in Vancouver. Originally from France, Bréchault graduated in photography at Emily Carr College of Art and Design and later turned to jewellery. Her photographic images in metal quietly suggest the feelings of someone with a French cultural background living on the West Coast. Her see-through acrylic suitcase, with alphabet letters, represents the trauma of cultural displacement that many new Canadians face.

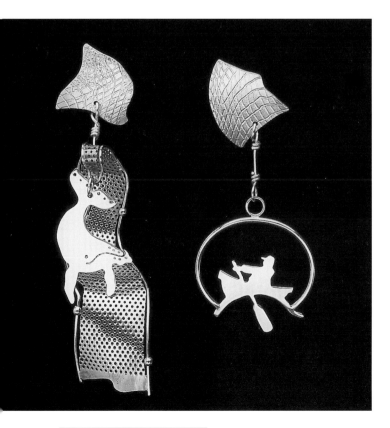

For many woman jewellers, feminist issues were at the forefront in the nineties. In a provocative body of work entitled *Plotting Our Progress/l'Etat de la Femme,* Montreal jeweller Barbara Stutman took on important feminist concerns in 1993. Stutman, while acknowledging her debt to Arline Fisch and Mary Lee Hu, used the textile techniques she had learned as a child from her grandmother in very graphic ways. Her most disturbing image, a neckpiece entitled *Raped* (Plate 49), dramatizes the trauma of the rape victim in a splayed and shackled spool-knit silver doll. The piece had no buyers — although it was beautifully crafted, its message made it unwearable — but it succeeded as a stark representation of Stutman's anger. The exhibit dealt more humorously with other issues of importance to women in the nineties, including body image and plastic surgery. Her *Tampon Holders* and

Assembly Line Breasts revealed a pungent sense of fun and colour in a challengingly literal presentation of ideas. They also reflected changes in the imagery used in jewellery as more women were designing and making it.

Lise Fortin's experiences of pregnancy became themes for two bodies of work: *Women and Their Pregnancy* and *African Arts (Mothering and Pregnancy).* For Fortin, a graduate of George Brown College and the Collège de Sainte-Foy, jewellery provides a very serious way to express intimate feelings. Her sterling silver pregnant ladies (Figs. 79 + 80) are curvaceous and animated, portraying the female form in the exuberance of childbearing. These pieces, while firmly descended from modern art, recall historical fertility symbols, and encode contemporary woman's understanding of her role in one of life's central events.

Fig. 78. │ D o m i n i q u e B r é c h a u l t │ Cultural Baggage (pendant), 1992, acrylic, copper, sterling silver, patinated, fabricated, 5.5 x 7.5 x 1.5 cm.

Fig. 80. │ L i s e   F o r t i n │ brooch, 1994, sterling silver, wood, 7 cm. high.

Beth M. Biggs, a graduate of NSCAD and the State University of New York at New Paltz, uses signs and symbols to express her ideas on gender. In a 1995 exhibition at the Art Gallery of Nova Scotia entitled *Stars are Suns,* Biggs showed six neckpieces and six "sun bowls". The bowls were of raised and sunk copper, with radiating elements that were cut and spread (for an example, see Fig. 81). Accompanying the presentation was an audio recording of a crackling fire. Biggs, like many smiths, attempts to imbue meaningful objects with historical associations that are significant to contemplate in a contemporary context.

In her MFA show at NSCAD, Beth Alber's questioning of jewellery from a feminine perspective led to work of conscious ambiguity. She exhibited large blackened-steel forms and showed in photographs how they might be worn on the body (Fig. 82). The pieces pointed to jewellery as a sign of male ownership and protection and, simultaneously, to woman's entrapment in set societal roles. Alber offered the following commentary: "I realized that women's roles are complex and full of contradictions. In our silence we have been active partners." Alber also exhibited finely crafted sterling silver wire cuffs that suggested wire cages. The cuffs were so small that their edges would dig

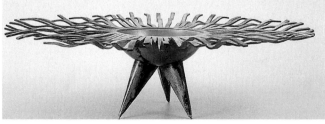

into the skin. Alber intended for gallerygoers to be reminded of history's pinching and crimping of women in the name of beauty. She was surprised to overhear many young visitors saying, "cool."

Societal debate over what constitutes pornography and erotica provoked an adventurous MAG Ontario show committee to choose *Taking Tea with Eros* as the theme for its 1994/95 exhibition. The exhibition's many depictions of sensuality were a departure from the jeweller's conventional hearts-and-flowers approach to eros. The jury unanimously selected Jackie Anderson's brooch, entitled *Was it good for you too?* (Fig. 83), as best-in-show. Like many other jewellery pieces, this needed to be handled to be fully appreciated. Its clasp was hidden by cutouts of discarded lingerie. The stones — lapis lazuli, rutilated quartz, moonstone and hematite — were chosen for their symbolism of love and night. Other entries portrayed the human figure in many guises, from cast and carved to fabricated shakudo and photo image.

Fig. 82.   B e t h   A l b e r   Propinquity, 1994, installation, steel forms, Nova Scotia College of Art and Design.

Fig. 83. ⏐ J a c k i e A n d e r s o n ⏐ Was it good for you too? (pin/pendant), 1994, sterling silver, hematite, lapis lazuli, moonstone, rutilated quartz, fabricated, 6.4 x 4.8 x 0.7 cm.

Lenka Suchanek's seated women showed a new direction in the use of textile techniques (Fig. 84). Her two figures, with long crimped hair, were made of tatted, handmade bobbin lace of copper wire stretched on a frame. Walter Schluep's entry in the show, ten erotic coins, received an award of excellence. Schluep, born in Spain and trained in Switzerland, came to Montreal in 1954. Schluep readily admits to having a one-track mind about jewellery. He believes that art should be compulsive and reflect the subconscious. His nineties jewellery is representational, depicting faces, female figures, and birds. His female figures are first intricately carved into stone and then cast in 18-karat gold (for an example, see Fig. 85). In his whim-sical *Crazy Bird* (Fig. 86), gold feet are added to a silver body. Schluep claims that he has made over ten thousand pieces of jewellery in his long career of exhibitions and commissions.

Magnum Opus was the grand title for a 1993 exhibition sponsored by MAG Ontario. The best-in-show award went to James Robson, Coordinator of the Jewellery Arts Department of George Brown College. Born and raised in Saskatoon, Robson, in his imagery, often reflects the diversity of the Canadian landscape. A 1987 brooch enti-tled *Well, Maybe One More Cow* (Fig. 87) shows the lonely cast critter as an icon of the west up against city life. A 1987 piece called *Nancy Drew Comes to the Big City* (Fig. 88) features the young detective against a

Fig. 84. | L e n k a   S u c h a n e k | Waiting for You I, Waiting for You II, 1994, tatted, handmade bobbin-lace copper wire, 20 x 25 x 20 cm.

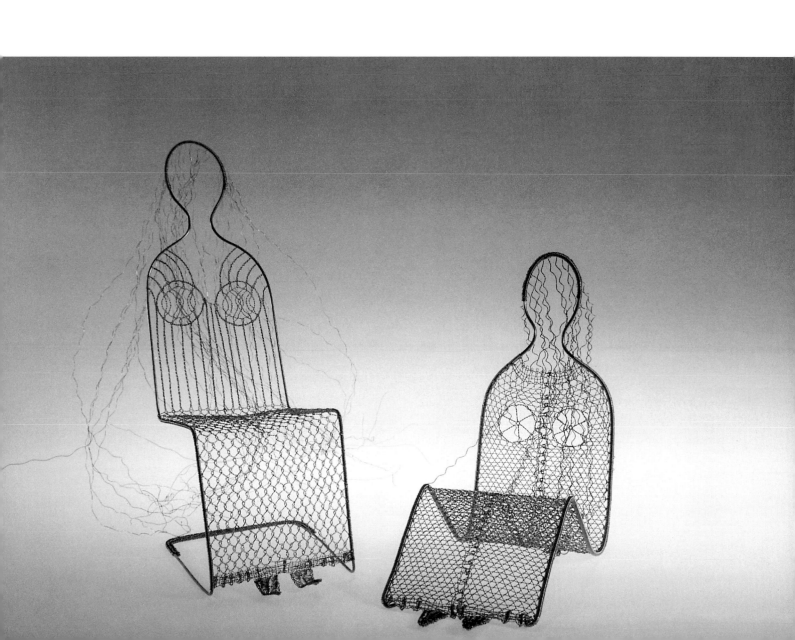

backdrop of grid-like office towers. Finally, in *Pound Sterling*, Robson fabricates the grid structure into a hollow tubular neckpiece with a ball that runs through it (Fig. 89). The piece, which weighed exactly one pound, went to the collection of the Canadian Museum of Civilization, in Hull, Quebec, as part of a 1992 agreement between the Museum and MAG Ontario. (The Canadian Museum of Civilization contains this country's most respectable collection of modern Canadian jewellery and metal art, which includes the Bronfman, Chalmers, Massey and Ontario Crafts Council collections. Other collections include the Winnipeg Art Gallery, which aims to acquire twentieth-century functional objects in ceramics, glass and silver by artists working in a studio environment; the Saskatchewan Art Bank; the Nova Scotia Permanent Collection; the Musée des Beaux Arts de Montréal; and the Musée de Civilisation du Québec.)

The design award for *Magnum Opus* was presented to Wendy Shingler, of Toronto, a graduate of St. Martin's School of Art, in London, for a neckpiece called *Foxfire* (Fig. 90). Matte-patinated brass

rings, combined with their cut-out inner circles, were joined together with silver wire in a complex layering of forms. Shingler's exploratory approach to metal has won her many design awards.

Faith Layard, a graduate of the University of Guelph and the Ontario College of Art, won the hollowware award and an award of excellence at *Magnum Opus*. The two winning pieces complemented each other, with similar arching forms. The use of enamel on her brooch *Arc to Woods* (see Plate 50) offered Layard's interpretation of nature not only through space and direction, but also through colour.

In 1994, the new Canadian Craft Museum, in Vancouver, collaborated with the Diamond Information Centre to host a competition entitled *Beyond Tradition: A Union of Diamonds and Craft*. Entrants were asked to "go beyond using traditional jewellery materials and techniques." They responded with such materials as duck wings, twigs, driftwood and a rusty chain. One of the twenty Canadian designers who won top honours was Lyn Strelau, of Calgary, the founder and owner of Jewels by Design. Strelau created a bangle of pure meteorite

Fig. 85. | W a l t e r   S c h l u e p | brooch, 1992, 18-karat gold, negative carving.

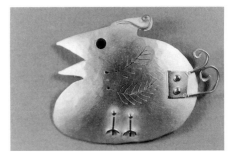

Fig. 86. | W a l t e r   S c h l u e p | Crazy Bird (brooch), 1991, sterling silver, 18-karat gold, fabricated.

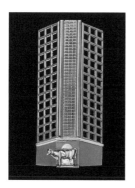

Fig. 87. [J a m e s   R o b s o n] Well, Maybe One More Cow (brooch), 1987, sterling silver, 18-karat gold, shakudo, shibuichi, cast, fabricated, 8 x 3 cm.

Fig. 88. [J a m e s   R o b s o n] Nancy Drew Comes to the Big City (brooch), 1987, sterling silver, surgical steel, cast, fabricated, gold plated, black rhodium plated, 4.5 x 7.5 cm.

Fig. 89. [J a m e s   R o b s o n] Pound Sterling (neckpiece), 1993, sterling silver, 900 gold, gold plated, fabricated, cast, 17 x 30 cm. Photo: Jeremy Jones.

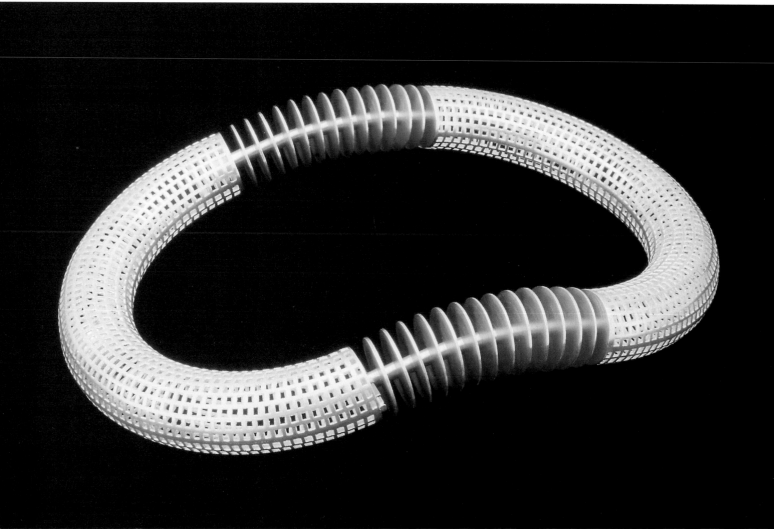

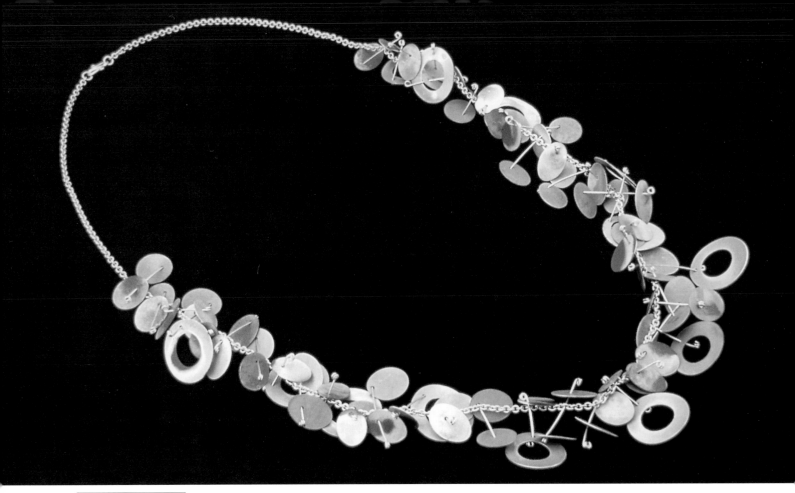

Fig. 90. **Wendy Shingler** **Foxfire** (neckpiece), 1992, brass, sterling silver, roller printed, patinated, fabricated, 38 x 10 cm. Photo: Jeremy Jones.

with champagne and white diamonds, which he called *Heaven and Earth*. The beauty and colour of gems that has lured so many to jewellery both as makers and collectors is stronger than ever in the nineties, and Strelau, Carl Torode, of Vancouver, and Gloria Bass, of Montreal, all of whom use gemstones and pearls, are among frequent winners in national and international jewellery competitions.

The trend toward colour and sculpture in hollowware has continued in the nineties. In 1993, Mark Peabody, of Kingston, Ontario, had a solo show entitled *Self Contained*. Peabody's architectural approach to hollowware is often inspired by late-nineteenth-century industrial buildings, with their exposed beams, brackets and rivets. Using wood with copper and steel, he makes containers that are more aesthetic than functional (see Fig. 91). The use of patinated metals by Peabody and others is not always for colour itself but points to an awareness of change and the effects of time. Quickening the aging process of metals with applied patinas connects today's work with historical pieces and reflects the feeling at the end of the century that all is not bright and shiny. In fact, all is complex and layered.

Fig. 91. │ M a r k P e a b o d y │ container, 1991, copper, steel, brass, purple heart, bloodwood, wenge, constructed, 11 x 20 cm.

106

In her hollowware, Brigitte Clavette, head of the jewellery department at the New Brunswick College of Craft and Design, is inspired by mechanical forms. For a 1991 exhibition entitled *Vestigium,* she created a small drum-like container with an amethyst ball stopper (Fig. 92). Supported by curving rods, the container's strength lies in its blunt forms. According to Clavette, the piece was made in response to her brother's death, and "recalls the life and death processes of decay and regeneration." Clavette placed a hidden inner container inside the drum to suggest soul or spirit within the exterior body.

In a large show that opened at the Muttart Gallery in Calgary in 1994, Jeff de Boer, a graduate of the Alberta College of Art, playfully considered the "need for armour in our modern world." He created finely articulated suits of mouse armour for mice of various historical periods (see Fig. 93). The silver suits featured decorative elements in brass, bronze and fabric, depending on the period. A book entitled *Articulation* tells the story of de Boer, his work, and his appreciative audience.

Combining jewellery with other art forms is a growing trend. Lucie Lambert, of Vancouver, combines her jewellery making with publishing. Lambert, born in Quebec, studied Chinese and Arab calligraphy in Paris. She then studied jewellery and carving under Bill Reid after she moved to the West Coast in 1983. Lambert publishes books that feature writers' and poets' responses to her own prints. Gradually she has incorporated silver medallions into the books. She has also begun a series of bracelets with engraved leaf designs (for an example, see Fig. 94). The leaves are pierced to accentuate the fluidity of their natural veining.

Fig. 94. | L u c i e L a m b e r t | bracelet, 1995, sterling silver, engraved, fabricated.

Fig. 93. | J e f f d e B o e r | Joan of Arc Mouse, 1995, brass, nickel, articulated, fabricated, chased, 10 x 5 cm. Photo: Ken Woo.

Crys Harse, a fibre and basket artist from Calgary, has joined
metal and natural fibres and pushed boundaries in both media. She
offers innovative workshops in sinking woven forms, raising wrinkled
metal (see Fig. 95), and creating "grass braids" of metal. For a 1996
Harbourfront exhibition entitled *Risk,* Tracy Lee, a graduate of OCA,
borrowed from the confectioner. Lee dipped sterling silver wire forms
in chocolate and displayed them in paper cups as if it were an enticing
box of candy (Fig. 96).

Fig. 95.   C r y s   H a r s e   Harnessed (vessel), 1994, brass, oak, leather, waxed linen, sinking, fabricated, 28 x 28 x 22.5 cm.

Fig. 96. Tracy Lee Assorted **1996**, 1996, sterling silver, bittersweet chocolate, fabricated, dipped. Photo: Ed Gatner.

Todd Tyarm, of Vancouver, is credited by Robert Lee Morris with inventing a new form of jewellery — the "Uroboros." Tyarm, who studied at the San Francisco Art Institute and moved to Canada in 1991, uses soft strips of leather to weave holders for artifacts that include a Pleistocene Age horse tooth, a chalcopyrite egg and a perfect specimen of smoky quartz (see Fig. 97). The Uroboros, with its woven construction, represents the endless cycle of life.

In this last decade of the twentieth century, Canadian jewellers are beginning to exhibit more and more internationally. Canadians have been regularly included in international shows such as Germany's *Ornamenta* and *Schmuckszene* exhibitions. In 1995, Stella Chan, of Gallery Suk Kwan, in Montreal, was the first gallery owner to take a large show of Canadian jewellery to Paris for exhibition in a French gallery.

In 1991, Ken Vickerson, a graduate of the Alberta College of Art and a teacher at OCA, participated in an exchange of goldsmiths between Karlsruhe, Germany, and Ontario. While in Germany he made *Totem,* a brooch based on a fantasy landscape (Plate 51). To Vickerson, metalsmithing techniques have provided a wide range of possibilities for relating personal images.

In 1992, Paul McClure, a graduate of NSCAD, participated in *Joies Indissenyables,* in Spain. McClure is concerned with jewellery as a socially interactive and communicative art form. His intriguing tubular forms resemble internal organs (see Fig. 98). To McClure, "the body is an extremely complex site for artistic expression." While heart imagery has become banal in jewellery, McClure's heart pendant (from his *Memento Mori* series), which resembles a real heart, was a challenging idea (Fig. 99). His use of blackened silver and pearls, a reference to historical mourning jewellery, reminds the viewer of human mortality. The coherence of McClure's work is compelling.

Simon Muscat, of Toronto, has had his sculptural jewellery exhibited at galleries in Europe and the United States. His one-of-a-kind bracelets (see Fig. 100) are carved in wax, hollowcast, and then fused together. Muscat says that his "aim is for a connectedness or unity."

Canada's first national museum dedicated to craft, the Canadian Craft Museum, in downtown Vancouver, reflects the growing stature of crafts in this country. Its inaugural exhibition, *A Treasury of Canadian Craft,* featured jewellery, hollowware, flatware and enamel. In her foreword to the exhibition catalogue, which offered historical and regional essays on Canada's craft history, Doris Shadbolt noted that while much of today's art is "message-driven" and "directed to the mind," craft revels in the material and the aesthetic. The beautiful, crafted object, with its direct sensual appeal, is the ideal sought by many metalworkers today.

Fig. 97. | Todd Tyarm | Uroboros Bag, 1995, leather, turquoise, Columbian quartz points, smoky quartz wand, bluejay feathers, 21.5 cm. long.

Fig. 98. Paul McClure pendant, 1991, sterling silver, copper, rubber, fabricated, 5.5 x 4 x 4 cm.

Fig. 99. Paul McClure Heart (pendant), Memento Mori series, 1994, sterling silver, pearl, fabricated, oxidized, 5 x 5 x 2.5 cm.

Fig. 100. Simon Muscat bracelet, 1986, sterling silver, hollow cast, fused, 9 x 9 x 4 cm.

Fig. 101. | Valerie Crowther | Snow Fence, 1992, sterling silver, fused, 2.5 x 5 cm.

Influences

What influences the conception and development of ideas in Canadian jewellery and metal today? Responses to this question from the metalsmithing community reveal that the environment, either natural landscape or constructed cityscape, is the primary source of inspiration.

Many artists, including Josée Poulin, are inspired by an urban landscape. Poulin says, "Canada is so big that it is hard for me to relate to it. I am more concerned about Montreal." For Valerie Crowther, the prairies have had a profound effect on her work (see Fig. 101). Beth Biggs, of Nova Scotia, judges that the "lifestyle of the Maritimes is very conducive to the art-making process," and Stevi Kittleson, from Hornby Island, in British Columbia, admits that she is a child of the West Coast and that her pieces strongly reflect an affinity with nature." For Charles Lewton-Brain, who has spent time in the Arctic, observations of the weathering and the metamorphosis of human and natural patterns (Fig. 102) have had a great impact on his work.

Other jewellers search outside Canada for inspiration. Anne Fauteux seeks out other cultures that will lead her to an international awareness. Ghislaine Fauteux-Langlois spent two years in West Africa, where she immersed herself in primitive African art and found inspiration in masks, tools and religious objects.

Still other jewellers have come to Canada from abroad. Britta Klingenstierna, originally from Sweden, enjoys Canada's cultural and ethnic mix, which, she believes, creates an "interesting fusion" of design. If she had stayed in Sweden, minimalist design would surely have been her main influence.

Fig. 102. | Charles Lewton-Brain | Arctic Pins, 1983, steel, sterling silver, 24-karat gold, doublée technique, 7 cm. in diameter each. Photo: Jeremy Jones.

Another acknowledged source of inspiration is the metalsmith's own life. Cathy McElroy says: "My work is about who I am and is rooted in my emotional self." Dee Fontains writes: "My work reflects a love of self." James Doran states: "the voices in my head tell me what art to make."

A third group of jewellers finds inspiration in the materials. Eric Leyland says that he is process driven as opposed to concept driven. He simply enjoys making things. For Doreen Lapointe, "The physical properties of metal are intriguing." To Robert Hicks it is the metal itself, even though refined, that offers the possibility for collaboration with nature.

Postmodernism continues to inform metalsmithing in the nineties. Perhaps the most significant influence of this movement on Canadian metalwork has been in its emphasis on content or meaning. Where modernism's emphasis on form and function was often anti decorative, the postmodern aesthetic demands references outside the object and invites the maker to use images and figures.

In jewellery, the personal has again become the ideal. After experiments with performance and installation art in the eighties, the nineties was a period of retrenchment. Nineties jewellery often features rich, low-lustre surfaces and is pared down in design. It frequently tells the tale of the maker. This trend may be partially influenced by American narrative jewellery. Nineties exhibitions have revealed that preciousness can be found not only in materials, but also in ideas and execution. Artists are free to express their observations on every aspect of life, from birth to death, in formal or conceptual ways.

In nineties objects, as with jewellery, postmodernism, with its historical buttresses, brought new collaborations with architects and designers, who, after decades of machined stainless steel, revelled in a market of patinated objects. The best Canadian metalwork of the nineties, however, rather than reflecting period influences of style, by its complexity and layering, promotes an emotional engagement with the viewer and expresses a period of economic and artistic anxiety.

Fig. 103. James Robson Working the Lower Bow, 1993, sterling and reticulation silver, 18-karat gold, roller printed, 4 x 6 cm. Photo: Jeremy Jones.

In many ways, through their juried shows, workshops, lectures, and newsletters, the metal guilds of Canada have achieved their goal of promoting metal art. As volunteer organizations, some have also struggled in weathering the vicissitudes of fundraising and membership participation. Even so, they have kept alive a forum in which interested craftspeople can contact each other and be stimulated. Much credit is due to MAG Ontario for its enviable record of almost fifty years of annual exhibitions in which the juries often rewarded innovation.

Juried and curated shows by metal guilds, craft councils, and galleries have been a good record of the changing metal scene in Canada. Although photographic and written documentation is scarce for the forties and the fifties, small metal organizations in divergent parts of the country presented their members' work to best advantage to distinguish it from both mass-produced and poorly made craft fare. Metalwork made strong showings in national multimedia exhibitions during the fifties and sixties, particularly because of the influx of master jewellers from Europe after the Second World War. Seventies exhibitions saw the emergence of graduates from broadened college programs. Their work showed an interest in experimentation and a command of a wide range of metalworking techniques. By the eighties, exhibitions were well documented photographically and were often accompanied by catalogues. They marked an increased professionalism in the art-jewellery community. With the strong influence of the new jewellery movement in England and Europe, alternative materials and coloured metals won awards. Nineties exhibitions heralded a return to precious materials, along with a concern for environmental and social issues.

The exhibition record also demonstrates how metal responded to design and art influences. From the 1940s to the 1960s, Scandinavian modern design was dominant, especially in hollowware. In jewellery, there were expressions of other modern art movements in biomorphic and constructivist pieces. The seventies were more eclectic. Some jewellers explored materials with an organic sculptural approach while others turned to more hard-edged geometric forms. By the eighties, minimalism informed much design thinking, and metalsmiths enjoyed exploring new materials. Where jewellery had always been considered mainly as ornament, in the eighties jewellery pushed boundaries to assert itself as object, and jewellers sought acceptance in the art world. Education played a large role in moving metalcraft to the point where it is now preoccupied with ideas usually associated with art.

Postmodern thinking has encouraged jewellers to seek inspiration in their own past. This has resulted in a new concern for ornamentation and personal expression. Although studio jewellers have usually been quick to interpret art and design movements, many metalsmiths approach their work from a personal standpoint that cannot be traced to any identifiable source.

Even before Ontario silversmith Douglas Boyd demanded that the world acknowledge that Canadians do more than raise mink, Canadian jewellers and metalsmiths grappled with whether Canadian metal art reflects an image of Canada. The most straightforward way that an image of Canada is reflected in metalwork is through the use of native Canadian materials, such as agates from Nova Scotia, ammonite from Alberta and the bone and hair of native Canadian species. The art brut approach of some jewellers and the shaman imagery of others has been pointed to as distinctly Canadian, as have the imagery of West Coast and arctic Natives. For a period during the fifties and sixties, Quebec enamelwork was perceived as representative of that province's cultural identity. In the eighties and nineties, several Canadian metalsmiths began to charge their work with political and social commentary, confronting national issues of Cruise Missile testing, the environment and fishing rights.

But the size and cultural diversity of this country defy an identifiable Canadian style. Rather than reflecting an iconographic vision of Canada, contemporary gold and silversmiths want to express themselves as artists and contribute to the Canadian identity with imaginative metalwork. In the best makers, there is a personal imagery that transcends place.

The market has also played a considerable role in determining what Canadian art jewellers have produced. Hand-fabricated metal of unusual design has always been bought by a narrow audience sympathetic to the arts and architecture. The prosperous years following the Second World War built confidence in the studio jeweller who worked in precious metals and gemstones. By the sixties and seventies, silver jewellery increased in size, reflecting not only design influence, but also the expansionist spirit of the times and the relative low cost of the material. With inflated gold prices the eighties saw a rise in the use of anodized and patinated metals. The recession of the nineties not only cut deeply into jewellery sales but also engendered a certain commercialism in design. Prompted by the need for security in a period of economic cutbacks, precious metals and gemstones returned, though in a smaller format. The ability of studio jewellers to respond to the vagaries of the market and maintain artistic integrity has been well tested in recent years.

Amid the pulls of art and market, over the past fifty years, Canadian art jewellers have left a legacy of excellent metalwork that has shown innovation in materials and imagination in design and personal expression. This body of work reflects technical expertise and artistic concern for form, space, colour and idea. Some of it challenges the role of jewellery in society, as well as perceptions of personal adornment.

International exhibitions and publications have underscored the fact that although Canadian output has not been prolific, it does merit attention. As art, Canadian metalsmithing has stood up to scrutiny of its aesthetics and intentions. Canadian jewellers have benefitted from their own production with a kind of "makers' knowledge" that has arisen from creative activity.

Canadian metalsmithing has blossomed. In a remarkably brief period of time, with skills learned mostly from European immigrants, Canadian metalsmiths have begun to produce imaginative jewellery and hollowware. Given the challenges of a relatively small population with a vast geographic distribution, the results have been impressive. This is not to say that Canadian work could not show more risk. But Canadians are a moderate people, and this has shown through in our work.

To continue the established momentum for innovation and personal expression, the metalsmithing community is building on its shared values and is attempting to increase the cross-country dialogue that is facilitated through exhibitions, reviews and exchanges. The number of jewellers and metalsmiths who belong to metal organizations in Canada is heartening, and there are now thirteen full-time jewellery programs and many part-time opportunities for education in metal. Networking among the guilds and schools could also help to build a stronger sense of community.

We can only speculate on what the next fifty years will bring — what new art movements, what new metals and technological advances, what changes in the environment, society or politics. Will Canadian metalsmiths be able to maintain the energy and excitement for their craft-based art? I think yes.

List of Illustrations

Fig. 1. Nancy Meek Pocock, brooch, late 1940s.

Fig. 2. Wednesday-afternoon class at Andrew Fussell's home studio, Asquith Street, Toronto, c. 1945.

Fig. 3. Trademark of the Metal Arts Guild of Nova Scotia.

Fig. 4. Nancy Meek Pocock, rendering for neckpiece, 1940s.

Fig. 5. Rudy Renzius, teapot, c. 1931.

Fig. 6. Andrew Fussell, pewter tea set, late 1930s.

Fig. 7. Douglas Boyd, Box presented to Princess Elizabeth and the Duke of Edinburgh, 1951.

Fig. 8. Harold G. Stacey, raised bowl, 1949, sterling silver.

Fig. 9. Mr.and Mrs.Norman Anderson, design for kilt pin with cut and polished agate, 1967.

Fig. 10. Carl Poul Petersen, Corn pattern covered dish, 1954.

Fig. 11. Harold G. Stacey, coffee pot, 1950.

Fig. 12. Hero Kielman, teapot, 1960.

Fig. 13. Georges Delrue, brooch, 1945.

Fig. 14. Georges Delrue, brooch, 1945.

Fig. 15. Toni Cavelti, brooch, c.1965.

Fig. 16. Bill Reid, box with lid, 1964.

Fig. 17. Warren William Ottemiller, cocktail shaker, 1969.

Fig. 18. Tommia Vaughan-Jones (left) and unidentified woman at exhibition opening,
Royal Ontario Museum, 1962.

Fig. 19. Jacques Troalen, *Psyche*, 1974.

Fig. 20. Georges Schwartz, *Qui suis-je?*, 1985.

Fig. 21. Pat Hunt, brooch, 1971.

Fig. 22. Reeva Perkins, neckpiece, 1968.

Fig. 23. Reeva Perkins, brooch, 1975.

Fig. 24. Helga Palko, brooch, 1966.

Fig. 25. Aggie Beynon, perfume bottle, 1983.

Fig. 26. Sandra Noble Goss, neckpiece (detail), 1977.

Fig. 27. Kim Dickinson, brooch, 1979.

Fig. 28. James Evans, one of a series of nine brooches, 1981.

Fig. 29. Donald Stuart, neckpiece, 1976.

Fig. 30. Donald Stuart, presentation rendering for rose bowl commissioned to accompany
the Glenn Gould Prize awarded to Canadian composer R. Murray Schafer, 1987.

Fig. 31. Colleen McCallum, box, 1977.

Fig. 32. Vanessa Compton, *Dragon Going Under the Wave of Life* (ring), 1976.

Fig. 33. Christel E. Klocke, brooch, 1971.

Fig. 34. Lois E. Betteridge, *Spice Shaker*, 1977.

Fig. 35. Sue Parke, headdress, 1986.

Fig. 36. Theo Janson, Mask, 1981.

Fig. 37. Martha Sturdy, metal bracelets, 1980s.

Fig. 38. Kim Snyder, *Weeds in Stream* (bracelet), 1983

Plate 13. Richard Karpyshin, *Party Jewellery* (two of a series of brooches on photographs), 1983.

Plate 14. David Didur, *Medal for Dishonour* (neckpiece), 1983.

Plate 15. Paul Leathers, brooch, 1987.

Plate 16. Martha Glenny, *Entry Charm* (bracelet), 1987.

Plate 17. Jackie Anderson, *Eamons* (pin and stand), 1986.

Plate 18. Diane Hanson and *Oksana Kit*, wallpiece with removable shapes, 1986.

Plate 19. Shayne Kjertinge, brooch, 1988.

Plate 20. Akira Ikegami, neckpiece, 1983.

Plate 21. Brooke Baillie, brooch, 1987.

Plate 22. Brenda Bear Epp, three scarab pins on stand, 1988.

Plate 23. Anne Barros, *Kool-Aid Container*, 1988.

Plate 24. David Didur, *New Moon in Rimouski*, 1988.

Plate 25. Fay Rooke, *Autumn Garden Passage*, 1984.

Plate 26. Alan Perkins, *Massey Hall 1894* (drawing), 1984–85.

Plate 27. James Doran, *Check Mate*, 1989.

Plate 28. Kai Chan, bodypiece, 1984.

Plate 29. Louis Tortell, bracelet, 1984.

Plate 30. Tracy Bright, set of four pins (*House on a Hill, House in a Field, House on the Prairie, House in the Dark*), 1988.

Plate 31. Julie Hartman, *Shelter* (container), 1989.

Plate 32. Jackie Anderson, *Show Home* (pin and stand), 1986.

Plate 33. Lyn Wiggins, *Triplet* (earrings), 1992.

Plate 34. Janis Kerman, earrings, 1991.

Plate 35. Shelley Matthews Blair, brooch, 1991.

Plate 36. Charles Lewton-Brain, *Glasses*, 1988.

Plate 37. D. Marie Jardine, *Marriage Bowl*, 1992.

Plate 38. Mel Wolski, *Hockey Game #2* (detail), 1991.

Plate 39. Madeleine Dansereau, *Artemis* (neckpiece), 1987.

Plate 40. Luc Pilon, *Cause and Effects* (brooch), 1990.

Plate 41. Ann Lumsden, *In Case of Emergency*, 1991.

Plate 42. Susan Wakefield, bracelet from series *How My Garden Grows*, 1994.

Plate 43. Doreen Lapointe, *Pick a Pepper*, 1994.

Plate 44. Josée Desjardins, *Eruca Sativa* (brooch), 1994.

Plate 45. Josée Desjardins, *Nais Vulgare* (brooch), 1994.

Plate 46. Anne Fauteux, *Rouages de la Pensée* (set of three rings), 1994.

Plate 47. Anne Fauteux, *Détourneur de Doutes* (ring), 1992.

Plate 48. Michel-Alain Forgues, sculpture, 1991.

Plate 49. Barbara Stutman, *Raped* (neckpiece), 1993.

Plate 50. Faith Layard, *Arc to Woods* (brooch), 1992.

Plate 51. Ken Vickerson, *Totem* (brooch), 1991.

Compendium of Artists

 Neil Carrick Aird
designer, goldsmith
Kingston, Ontario
b. 1945 Dumbarton, Scotland
Educated at Glasgow School of Art
Active in Canada since 1968

Beth Alber, artist, teacher
Toronto, Ontario
b. 1942 Toronto, Ontario
Educated at Sheridan College School
of Design
Active in Canada since 1974

 Judith Almond-Best
Madoc, Ontario
b. 1944 Toronto, Ontario
Educated at Sheridan College School
of Design
University of Ottawa
Active in Canada 1968–82, 1993–

 Jackie Anderson
jeweller, designer, artist
Calgary, Alberta
b. 1953 Calgary, Alberta
Educated at Alberta College of Art
Active in Canada since 1975–

Guy Audette, jeweller, professor
Quebec, Quebec
b. 1953 Sillery, Quebec
Certificat Pedagogie
Active in Canada since 1975

Haakon Bakken, teaching master
Burlington, Ontario
b. 1932 Madison, Wisconsin
Educated at University of Wisconsin;
School for American Craftsmen,
Rochester, New York
Active in Canada 1967–85

Mary Anne Barkhouse
artist, metalsmith
Toronto, Ontario
b. 1961 Vancouver,
British Columbia
Educated at Ontario College of Art
Active in Canada since 1990

 Anne Barros, silversmith
Toronto, Ontario
b. 1939 Watertown, New York
Educated at College of New Rochelle;
Humber College
Active in Canada since 1975

George Bartel, metalsmith
Tatamagouche, Nova Scotia
b. 1943 Leipzig, Germany
Apprenticeship 1961–66
Active in Canada since 1961

 Gloria Bass, jeweller
Westmount, Quebec
b. 1950 Montreal, Quebec
Educated at McGill University
Apprenticed under John Blackwood,
Steven Brixner
Active in Canada since 1976

Beth Beattie, jeweller
Iqaluit, Northwest Territory
Educated at Arctic College
Active in Canada since 1995

Gilles Beaugrand, silversmith
Montreal, Quebec, b. 1906
Educated at École des
beaux-arts de Montréal;
three years' study in France
Active in Canada 1932–95

Laura Beazley, jewellery designer
Toronto, Ontario
Educated at George Brown College
Active in Canada since 1989

Frances Beis
jewellery designer, enamellist
Tantallon, Nova Scotia
b. 1937 Green Bay, Wisconsin
Educated at University of Wisconsin
Active in Canada since 1978

Sandra Bell
Calgary Alberta
b. 1949 Vermilion, Alberta
Educated at Alberta College of Art
Active in Canada since 1988

LEB Lois Etherington Betteridge
silversmith
Guelph, Ontario
b. 1928 Drummondville, Quebec
Educated at Ontario College of Art;
University of Kansas; Cranbrook
Academy of Art
Member Royal Canadian Academy
Active in Canada 1952–61, 1967 –

Aggie Beynon, jeweller
Waterloo, Ontario
b. 1947 Hamilton, Ontario
Educated at University of Kansas;
University of Waterloo
Active in Canada since 1985

Beth Biggs, jeweller
Aspotogan, Nova Scotia
b. 1961 Deep River, Ontario
Educated at Algonquin College; Nova
Scotia College of
Art and Design; State University of
New York at New Paltz
Active in Canada since 1983

 John Blair, jewellery artist
Calgary, Alberta
b. 1952 Ottawa, Ontario
Educated at Alberta College of Art
Active in Canada since 1972

Ronald Bloore, artist
Toronto, Ontario
b. 1925 Brampton, Ontario
Educated at University of Toronto;
New York University; Washington
University, St. Louis, Missouri;
Courtault Institute,
University of London
Active in Canada since 1958

Barry Blunden
coppersmith, tinsmith
Kingston, Ontario
b. 1948 Kingston, Ontario
Educated at St. Lawrence College;
George Brown College;
Algonquin College
Active in Canada since 1965

Douglas Boyd
Richmond Hill, Ontario
b. 1901 Toronto, Ontario
d. 1972 Richmond Hill, Ontario
Active in Canada 1936–72

Kate Bradbury, metalsmith
Hampton, New Brunswick
b. 1967 the Shetland Islands, U.K.
Educated at Queen's University;
Georgian College; Nova Scotia College
of Art and Design
Active in Canada since 1992

Jacques Bradet
Sainte-Madeleine, Quebec
Active in Canada since 1990

Maurice Brault, jeweller
Montreal, Quebec
b. 1930 Montreal, Quebec
Educated at École des Beaux-Arts de
Montréal; École Superieure
d'Architecture et des Arts Decoratifs
de l'Abbaye de la Cambre, Brussels,
Belgium; Atelier Leroux-
Guillaume, Montreal; Firme Tostrup,
Oslo, Norway
Active in Canada 1957–72,
1985–88
Collection of drawings, jewellery and
holloware shown at the Museum of
Civilization of Québec, 1995.

Dominique Bréchault, jeweller
Vancouver, British Columbia
b. 1953 Thouars, France
Educated at Vancouver Community
College; Emily Carr
College of Art and Design; University
of Poitiers, France
Active in Canada since 1991

Arthur Leroy Brecken
Erin, Ontario
b. 1915 Toronto, Ontario
Educated at Mount Allison University
Active in Canada since 1938

Indira Breiter-Noro, jeweller
Agincourt, Ontario
b. 1966 Toronto, Ontario
Educated at George Brown College
Active in Canada since 1985

Morgan Bristol, jeweller
Tlell, British Columbia
b. 1955 Seattle, Washington
Educated at Alberta College of Art
Active in Canada since 1981

Mark Brose, designer, jeweller
Toronto, Ontario
b. 1962 Kenora, Ontario
Educated at Ontario College of Art
George Brown College
Active in Canada since 1984

Clifford Brown, jeweller
Halifax, Nova Scotia
By appointment, Jeweller to Queen
Elizabeth, the Queen Mother, 1939

Karen Anderson Cantine
silversmith
Edmonton, Alberta
b. 1941 Cambridge, Massachusetts
Educated at University of Iowa
Active in Canada since 1979

CARNAT Sarabeth Carnat, artist, jeweller
Calgary, Alberta
b. 1949 Calgary, Alberta
Educated at the New School of Art,
Toronto; Sheridan
College School of Design; Bezalel
Academy of Art and
Design, Jerusalem, Israel; Nova Scotia
College of Art and Design
Active in Canada since 1969

 Toni Cavelti, jeweller
Vancouver, British Columbia
b. 1931 Switzerland
Educated at Vancouver School of Art
Apprenticed in St. Gallen, Switzerland
Active in Canada since 1954

Madeleine David Chagnon
enamellist, sculptor
Ste-Anne-des-Lacs, Quebec
b. 1934, Montreal, Quebec
Educated at Université du
Québec à Montréal
Active in Canada since 1974

Kai Chan, artist
Toronto, Ontario
b. China 1940
Educated at Chung Chi College, Hong
Kong; Ontario College of Art; Banff
School of Fine Arts
Active in Canada since 1982

 Bernard Chaudron, pewtersmith
Val-David, Quebec
b. 1931 Lille, France
Educated in agriculture and art,
Reims, France
Active in Canada since 1960

Linda Chow, goldsmith, designer
Calgary, Alberta
b. 1948 Hong Kong
Educated at Alberta College of Art
Active in Canada since 1972

 Brigitte Clavette, metalsmith
CLAVETTE Fredericton, New Brunswick
b. 1956 St. Basile, New Brunswick
Educated at Nova Scotia College of Art
and Design
Active in Canada since 1980

Kelly Clemmer
Wainwright, Alberta
b. 1971 Wainwright, Alberta
Educated at Alberta College of Art
Active in Canada since 1991

 Susan Cockburn
Toronto, Ontario
b. 1959 Toronto, Ontario
Educated at University of Toronto;
Sheridan College
Active in Canada since 1980

 Nathaniel Cohen
Dartmouth, Nova Scotia
b. 1926 London, England
Self-taught
Active in Canada since 1985

 Vanessa Compton
jewellery designer
Hamilton, Ontario
b. 1952 Montreal, Quebec
Educated at Concordia University;
Sheridan College School of Design;
University of Waterloo
Active in Canada since 1972

Jo-Anne Critchley Browne
craftsperson
Matheson, Ontario
b. 1950 Toronto
Educated at Sheridan College School
of Design
Active in Canada since 1974

 Valerie Crowther, goldsmith
Regina, Saskatchewan
b. 1952 Alliston, Ontario
Educated at Sheridan College School
of Design;
George Brown College
Active in Canada since 1974

 Peter Cullman, goldsmith
Toronto, Ontario
b. 1941 Berlin
Apprenticed at Idar-Oberstein,
Germany. Further studies at Kunst &
Werkschule, Pforzheim, Germany
Active in Canada since 1977

 Peter Currie, metalsmith
Toronto, Ontario
b. 1967 Guelph, Ontario
Apprenticed under Lois Betteridge
Educated at George Brown College
Active in Canada since 1986

Ivi Daborn, jeweller
Wolfville, Nova Scotia
b. 1943 Rakvere, Estonia
Educated at Concordia University;
University of Alberta; Acadia
University
Active in Canada since 1975

 Gertrude Daignault, jeweller
Montreal, Quebec
b. 1941 Missisquoi, Quebec
Educated at CEGEP du Vieux
Montréal; École de Joaillerie et de
Métaux d'Art
de Montréal
Active in Canada since 1980

Peter Danes, designer
Toronto, Ontario
b. 1946 Czechoslovakia
Educated at School for Applied Arts,
Prague; School for Industrial Design,
Prague
Active in Canada since 1989

Madeleine Dansereau, jeweller
b. 1922,
d. 1991 Montreal, Quebec
Educated at École des Beaux-Arts
de Montréal; Université
du Québec à Montréal
Apprenticed under Philippe Vauthier
Co-founder of École de Joaillerie et de
Métaux d'Art de Montréal

 Ann Davern, jeweller
Vancouver, British Columbia
b. 1930 Ottawa, Ontario
Workshop educated
Active in Canada since 1961

Robert Davidson, artist
Masset, British Columbia
b. 1946 Hydaburg, Alaska
Apprenticed with Bill Reid
Educated at Vancouver School of Art
Active in Canada since 1966

 Valerie Davidson, jeweller
Keene, Ontario
b. 1961 Peterborough, Ontario
Educated at Sheridan College School
of Craft and Design
Apprenticed under Libby Smith
Active in Canada since 1984

 Jeff de Boer, metalsmith
Calgary, Alberta
b. Calgary, Alberta
Educated at Alberta College of Art
Active in Canada since 1986

Bev de Jong, metal artist
Terra Cotta, Ontario
b. 1945 Calgary, Alberta
Educated at Alberta College of Art;
Cranbrook Academy of Art
Active in Canada since 1969

Alexandra Deliyannides, metalsmith
Calgary, Alberta
b. 1972 Alberta
Educated at Alberta College of Art
Active in Canada since 1990

 Georges Delrue
jeweller, silversmith
Val Morin, Quebec
b. 1920 Tourcoing, France
Apprenticed at Gabriel Lucas Joaillier,
Educated at École des Beaux-Arts de
Montréal; École du Meuble, Montreal
Active in Canada since 1947

Josée Desjardins, jeweller
Montreal, Quebec
b. 1963 Hull, Quebec
Educated at École de Joaillerie et de
Métaux d'Art de Montréal
Active in Canada since 1985

David Didur, metalsmith
Port Hope, Ontario
b. 1953 Saskatoon, Saskatchewan
Educated at Nova Scotia College of Art
and Design
Active in Canada since 1975

Amy Dona, jeweller
Ingersoll, Ontario
b. 1971 Ingersoll, Ontario
Educated at Georgian College
Active in Canada since 1993

125

James Doran, artist
Winnipeg, Manitoba
b. 1952 Vancouver,
British Columbia
Educated at University of Manitoba
Self-taught in enamel
Active in Canada since 1980

Willa McQueen Drummond
Toronto, Ontario
b. 1967 Montreal, Quebec
Educated at Ontario College of Art;
University of Western Ontario
Active in Canada since 1994

R. Melanie Egan, jeweller
Toronto, Ontario
b. 1959 Thunder Bay, Ontario
Educated at George Brown College
Active in Canada 1980–89

 David Elliott, artist
Montreal, Quebec
b. 1966 Canberra, Australia
Self-taught
Active in Canada since 1985

 Gillian Marie Escalante, designer
Vancouver, British Columbia
b. 1964 Vancouver, British Columbia
Educated at Vancouver Community
College; Emily Carr Institute
of Art and Design
Active in Canada since 1994

126

James Evans, teacher, critic
Brighton, England
b. 1952 Kingston, Ontario
Educated at George Brown College;
Nova Scotia College of
Art and Design
Active in Canada 1981–90

 Yvonne Evans, jewellery designer
Surrey, British Columbia
b. 1931 North Vancouver, British
Columbia
Active in Canada since 1955

 Ghislaine Fauteau-Langlois, artist
Hull, Quebec
b. 1941 Shawinigan, Quebec
Educated at École de Joaillerie et de
Métaux d'Art de Montréal; École
Nationale Supérieure des Arts
Décoratifs de Paris; Université du
Québec à Montréal
Active in Canada since 1984

 Anne Fauteux, jeweller, teacher
Montreal, Quebec
b. 1959 Ottawa, Ontario
Educated at Concordia University;
École de Joaillerie et de Métaux d'Art
de Montréal; Banff School of Fine Arts
Apprenticed under Manfredi Gioielli,
Varese, Italy; and under Gabriella
Rivalta, Casale Monferrato, Italy
Active in Canada since 1986

Gael Ferris
Toronto, Ontario
b. Vancouver, British Columbia
Educated at Boston University;
Ontario College of Art and Design
Active in Canada since 1995

Richard Finney, sculptor
Winnipeg, Manitoba
b. 1955 Winnipeg, Manitoba
Educated at University of Manitoba;
Sturgeon Creek Regional School
Active in Canada since 1980

Dee Fontans, artist, jeweller
Calgary, Alberta
b. 1958 East Orange, New Jersey
Educated at State University of
New York at New Paltz; Parsons
School of Design; the New School
of Social Research
Active in Canada since 1988

Michel Alain Forgues, jeweller
St. Lazare, Quebec
b. Lauzon, Quebec
Educated at Institut des Arts
Appliques, Montreal
Active in Canada since 1971

Lise Fortin, jeweller
Montreal, Quebec
b. 1958 Quebec
Educated at George Brown College;
École de Joaillerie et de Métaux d'Art
de Montréal; College de Sainte-Foy
Active in Canada since 1980

Ken Fox
Lower Sackville, Nova Scotia
b. 1922 Bedford, Nova Scotia
Took courses at Nova Scotia Centre
for Craft and Design; Metal Arts Guild
of Nova Scotia
Active in Canada since 1976

Lolly (Lois) Frankel, designer
Calgary, Alberta
b. 1951 Toronto, Ontario
Educated at Sheridan College School
of Design; Nova Scotia College of Art
and Design; University of Calgary;
Kunstakademie, Dusseldorf, Germany
Active in Canada 1980–84, 1994–

Douglas D. Frey
designer, goldsmith
Saskatoon, Saskatchewan
b. 1953 Leader, Saskatchewan
Educated at University of
Saskatchewan
Self-taught in jewellery
Active in Canada since 1975

Andreas Friderichsen, silversmith
Edmonton, Alberta
b. 1921 Denmark
Studied silversmithing
under Karen Cantine
Active in Canada since 1983

 FUSSEL Andrew Fussell,
b. 1904 Leipzig, Germany
d. 1983 Toronto, Ontario
Studied with Rudi Renzius at Northern
Vocational and
Technical School,

T.GALLAGHER Trudy Gallagher
Fredericton, New Brunswick
b. 1958 London, Ontario
Educated at Le Centre de Formation
Professionnelle, Quebec
Active in Canada since 1987

Jasmine Gardener, artist
Calgary, Alberta
b. 1971 Calgary, Alberta
Educated at Alberta College of Art
Active in Canada since 1989

Hans Gehrig
Montreal, Quebec
b. 1929 Zurich, Switzerland
d. 1981 Mendrisio, Switzerland
Apprenticed in Zurich and Basle
Active in Canada 1952–?

Bruno Gérard, jeweller, sculptor
Montreal, Quebec
b. 1953 Reims, France
Educated at École de Joaillerie et de
Métaux d'Art de Montréal; École de
Formation Professionelle de Québec
Active in Canada since 1983

Otto Gerendas
Toronto, Ontario
b. 1918
Educated at University of Toronto

JEG Jean-Eudes Germain, jeweller, sculptor
Montreal, Quebec
b. 1950 Quebec, Quebec
Educated at École de Joaillerie et de
Métaux d'Art de Montréal;
Université de Laval
Active in Canada since 1984

T/MG Martha Glenny, artist, goldsmith
Halifax, Nova Scotia
b. 1953 Fort Erie, Ontario
Educated at Nova Scotia College
of Art and Design;
George Brown College
Active in Canada since 1975

 Kevin Robert Gordon, jeweller
Winnipeg, Manitoba
b. Summerside, Prince Edward Island
Apprenticed under Stephen
Cole Powell
Active in Canada since 1981

 Nora L. Goreham, jeweller, teacher
Halifax, Nova Scotia
b. 1932 Shag Harbour, Nova Scotia
Educated at Mount Allison University
Studied pewter under Frances Felton
Active in Canada since 1960

Andrew Goss, jeweller
Owen Sound, Ontario
b. 1944 London, England
Educated at Hornsey College of Art,
London, England; George Brown
College; University of Toronto
Active in Canada since 1973

Gussie Gowans, jeweller
St. Catharines, Ontario
b. 1947 Bound Brook, New Jersey

James Green, jeweller
b. 1903 London, England
d. 1993 Burlington, Ontario
Apprenticed in London, England
Taught at Ryerson Polytechnical
Institute 1948–53
Active in Canada 1946–93

A.G. Anne Grotrian, jeweller
Toronto, Ontario
b. 1928 Toronto, Ontario
Educated at Ontario College of Art;
Instituto Allende, Mexico; George
Brown College
Active in Canada since 1977

 Dietje Hagedoorn, goldsmith
Bowen Island, British Columbia
b. 1952 Lochem, the Netherlands
Educated at Vakschool-Schoonhoven,
the Netherlands
Active in Canada since 1975

Kim Halfyard, metalsmith, jeweller
Toronto, Ontario
b. 1962 Montreal, Quebec
Educated at George Brown College
Active in Canada since 1990

 Lyn Haliburton, jeweller
Toronto, Ontario
b. 1956 Toronto, Ontario
Educated at Nova Scotia College of Art
and Design
Active in Canada since 1980

Diane Hanson
jeweller, manufacturer
Toronto, Ontario
b.1960 Toronto
Educated at Humber College; George
Brown College
Active in Canada since 1982

 Claudette Hardy-Pilon, jeweller
Montreal, Quebec
b. 1946 St. Félicien, Quebec
Educated at École de Joaillerie et
de Métaux d'Art de Montréal;
École des Beaux-Arts de Montréal
Active in Canada since 1979

Monica Harhay, jeweller
Toronto, Ontario
b. 1949 Toronto, Ontario
Educated at Ryerson
Polytechnical Institute; Sheridan
College School of Design
Active in Canada 1974–89

Crys Harse, metalsmith
Calgary, Alberta
b. 1939 London, England
Educated at Alberta College of Art and
Design
Active in metalsmithing since 1990

Julie Hartman, jeweller
Toronto, Ontario
b. 1961 Stratford, Ontario
Educated at Sheridan College
Active in Canada since 1985

Janet A. Hellerud, jeweller
Cumberland, British Columbia
b. 1947 Two Hills, Alberta
Educated at Vancouver City College;
Alberta College of Art
Active in Canada since 1991

HELLERUD

 Ginette Henri, jewellery designer
Moncton, New Brunswick
b. 1955 Acadiaville, New Brunswick
Educated at Community College,
Dieppe, New Brunswick
Active in Canada since 1989

Robert W. Hicks, artist
Lethbridge, Alberta
b. Williston, North Dakota
Educated at University of Washington;
California College of Arts and Crafts;
Minneapolis Art Institute
Active in Canada since 1976

Valarie Hudson, jeweller
Toronto, Ontario
b. 1955 Toronto, Ontario
Educated at Ontario College of Art;
George Brown College
Active in Canada since 1992

David Hunt, teacher
Newburgh, Ontario
b. 1943 St. Thomas, Ontario
Educated at Ontario College of Art
Active in Canada since 1967

 Pat Hunt, jeweller
Toronto, Ontario
b. 1911 Toronto, Ontario
Educated at George Brown College
Active in Canada 1958–88

Robert H. Hutchings
jewellery designer/manufacturer
Kingston, Ontario
b. 1931 London, England
Apprenticed in Gosport, England
Active in Canada since 1953

Akira Ikegami, jeweller, professor
Toronto, Ontario
b. 1939 Japan
Educated in fine arts, Japan; George
Brown College; Rochester Institute
of Technology
Active in Canada since 1969

 Lydia Ilarionova, designer
Montreal, Quebec
b. 1954 Sofia, Bulgaria
Educated at School of Fine and
Applied Arts, Sofia, Bulgaria,
Active in Canada since 1992

 Mary Janeway, metalsmith
Vancouver, British Columbia
b. 1949 Maracaibo, Venezuela
Educated at Emily Carr College of Art
and Design; University of British
Columbia
Self-taught in metal
Active in Canada since 1986

Theo Janson, jeweller
Desboro, Ontario
b. 1946 New Brunswick, New Jersey
Educated at University of Florida
Apprenticed under Frank X. Phillips
Active in Canada 1972–85

D. Marie Jardine, metalsmith
Halifax, Nova Scotia
b. 1962 Halifax, Nova Scotia
Educated at Nova Scotia College
of Art and Design
Active in Canada since 1988

LJ/ST Louise Olivia Jarvis, artisan, teacher
Kitchener, Ontario
b. 1948 Welland, Ontario
Educated at University of Guelph;
Mohawk College; Sheridan College
School of Design
Active in Canada since 1978

Janis D. Johnson, jeweller
Vancouver, British Columbia
b. 1955 Drumheller, Alberta
Educated at Alberta College of Art;
George Brown College
Active in Canada since 1982

 Kristen Jones, goldsmith
Vancouver, British Columbia
b. 1958 Vancouver, British Columbia
Educated at Emily Carr College of Art
and Design; Vancouver Community
College, Revere Academy,
San Francisco
Active in Canada since 1990

MJDS Megan Jones, goldsmith
Uxbridge, Ontario
b. 1952 Guelph, Ontario
Educated at George Brown College
Active in Canada since 1976

127

 Vivienne Jones, jeweller
Toronto, Ontario
b. 1955 Wales, U.K.
Educated at Swansea Art School, Wales;
Birmingham Polytechnic, England
Active in Canada since 1976

Enid Kaplan, artist
Montreal, Quebec
b. 1954 New York City
Educated at Rhode Island School of
Design; Instituto Fujimura, Florence
Active in Canada 1989–1991, 1994–

Richard Karpyshin, jeweller, sculptor
Winnipeg, Manitoba
b. 1955 Winnipeg, Manitoba
Educated at University of Manitoba;
Nova Scotia College of Art and Design
Active in Canada since 1982

William Kearns, gemmologist
St. John, New Brunswick
b. 1940 New Glasgow, Nova Scotia
Self-taught

Linda Keays, artist, teacher
Sudbury, Ontario
b. 1947 England
Educated at City of Belfast College of
Art, Northern Ireland; Melbourne
State College, Australia
Active in Canada since 1992

 Janis Kerman
jewellery designer/manufacturer
Westmount, Quebec
b. 1957 Montreal, Quebec
Educated at Boston University;
Washington University; Sheridan
College School of Design
Active in Canada since 1978

Hero Kielman
jeweller, teaching master
Toronto, Ontario
b. 1919 the Netherlands
Educated at Dutch Governmental
School of Arts and Crafts,
The Netherlands
Active in Canada since 1953

Oksana Kit, jewellery designer
Toronto, Ontario
b. 1954 Toronto, Ontario
Educated at George Brown College;
Ontario College of Art
Active in Canada since 1980

Stevi Parker Kittleson, jeweller
Hornby Island, British Columbia
b. 1948 San Francisco, California
Self-taught
Active in Canada since 1970

Shayne Kjertinge, artist
Toronto, Ontario
b. 1961 Etobicoke, Ontario
Educated at Ontario College of Art
Active in Canada 1988–94

Britta Klingenstierna
Westmount, Quebec
b. 1948 Stockholm, Sweden
Educated at Byam Shaw School of Art,
London, England; University of
Stockholm; École de Joaillerie et de
Métaux d'Art de Montréal
Active in Canada since 1993

128

Christel-Elvira Klocke, master gold and
silversmith, gemmologist
Toronto, Ontario
b. 1939 Berlin, Germany
Educated in Berlin
Active in Canada since 1964

Alfred Michael Korber
Toronto, Ontario
b. 1922 Vienna, Austria
Educated at Gewerbe Schule VI,
Techn. Werkmeister Schule I, Vienna
Active in Canada since 1953

DKTO
Dorota Kretowska, jewellery designer
North York, Ontario
b. 1962 Poland
Educated at George Brown
College; State Theater School,
Bialystok, Poland
Active in Canada since 1989

Debra Kuzyk, artist
Stephenville, Newfoundland
b. 1958 Cutknife, Saskatchewan
Educated at Nova Scotia College of Art
and Design; University of
Saskatchewan; Banff School of Fine Art
Active in Canada since 1988

Antoine D. Lamarche
designer, jeweller
Montreal, Quebec
b. 1939 Oissel, France
Educated at The Art Center, Lima,
Peru; École des Beaux Arts, Lima,
Peru; École des Beaux Arts, Montréal;
École de Joaillerie et de Métaux
d'Art de Montréal
Active in Canada since 1978

Lucie Lambert, artist, publisher
Vancouver, British Columbia
b. 1947 Shawinigan, Quebec
Educated at Université du
Québec à Montréal
Studied Haida carving with Bill Reid

Doreen Lapointe, metal artist
Winnipeg, Manitoba
b. 1965 Winnipeg, Manitoba
Educated at Nova Scotia College of Art
and Design; George Brown College;
Sturgeon Creek School, Winnipeg,
Manitoba. Apprenticed under Paul
Leathers, Winnipeg
Active in Canada since 1986

Kim Larsen, jeweller
Winnipeg, Manitoba
b. Winnipeg, Manitoba
Educated at George Brown College
Active in Canada since 1986

OMFL
LARSON
Orland Larson, goldsmith, educator
Mahone Bay, Nova Scotia
b. 1931 Shaunavon, Saskatchewan
Educated at University of
Saskatchewan; University of
Wisconsin; School for American
Craftsmen, Rochester, New York; Tyler
School of Art, Philadelphia; Columbia
University, New York
Apprenticed under Michael Murray,
London, England
Active in Canada since 1960

Robin Lavis, artist
Hornby Island, British Columbia
b. 1948 London, England
Self-taught
Apprenticed under Wayne Ngan and
Kurt Morrison
Active in Canada since 1989

Pgl
Peter Lawrence, designer, jeweller
Bridgetown, Nova Scotia
b. 1952 Halifax
Educated at Nova Scotia College of Art
and Design
Active in Canada since 1979

Faith Layard, enamellist, metalsmith
Campbellville, Ontario
b. 1963 Ontario
Educated at Ontario College of Art;
University of Guelph
Active in Canada since 1987

Paul Leathers, designer, goldsmith
Winnipeg, Manitoba
b. 1961 Winnipeg, Manitoba
Educated at Nova Scotia College of Art
and Design; Sheridan College School
of Craft and Design
Active in Canada since 1978

Michèle LeBleu, jeweller
Montreal, Quebec
b. 1947 Amos (Abitibi), Quebec
Educated at École de Joaillerie et de
Métaux d'Art de Montréal; Université
du Québec à Montréal

Tracy Lee, jeweller
Toronto, Ontario
b. Toronto 1969
Educated at Ontario College of Art
Active in Canada since 1992

Susan Rose Lefebour
goldsmith, jewellery designer
Toronto, Ontario
b. 1965 Bombay, India
Educated at George Brown College,
Nova Scotia College of Art and Design,
Apprenticed at Barbara Heinrich Studio
Active in Canada since 1994

Michael Letki, jeweller, teacher
Toronto, Ontario
b. 1945 Moreton-on-the-Marsh,
England Educated at Loughborough
College of Art and Design, England;
University of Toronto
Active in Canada since 1969

Paula Letki, artist, teacher
Toronto, Ontario
b. Warsop, England
Educated at Loughborough
College of Art and Design, England;
University of Toronto
Active in Canada since 1969

Paul M. Lewis, jeweller
Winnipeg, Manitoba
b. 1951 St. Boniface, Manitoba
Educated at University of Manitoba;
Niagara College of Applied Arts
and Technology; Bakketun
Ungdomskole, Verdal, Norway
Active in Canada since 1972

BRAIN
Charles Lewton-Brain
artist, goldsmith
Calgary, Alberta
b. 1956 London, England
Educated at State University of
New York at New Paltz;
Volkschochschule, Pforzheim,
West Germany; Nova Scotia College
of Art and Design; Sheridan College
School of Design; Ulster County
Community College, New York
Active in Canada since 1975

Eric Leyland, goldsmith, teacher
Nelson, British Columbia
b. 1955 Toronto, Ontario
Educated at George Brown College;
Ontario College of Art
Active in Canada since 1974

Claude Loranger, jeweller
Montreal, Quebec
b. 1954 Point-Viau, Quebec
Educated at École de Joaillerie et de
Métaux d'Art de Montréal; Collège
Edouard-Monpetit, Longueuil
Active in Canada 1979–91

Ann Lumsden, goldsmith
Kingston, Ontario
b. 1963 Ottawa, Ontario
Educated at George Brown College;
Carleton University
Active in Canada since 1986

Sylvie Lupien, jeweller
Montreal, Quebec
b. 1960 Berthierville, Quebec
Self-taught
Active in Canada since 1985

Kimberley A. MacHardy Mitman
Butte, Montana
b. 1964 Halifax, Nova Scotia
Educated at Nova Scotia College
of Art and Design
Active in Canada 1985–93

Ted Maciurzynski
architect, goldsmith
Winnipeg, Manitoba
b. 1959 Winnipeg, Manitoba
Educated at University of Manitoba
Self-taught metalsmith
Active in Canada since 1978

 Wayne Mackenzie
designer, goldsmith
Edmonton, Alberta
b. 1947 Mannville, Alberta
Educated at Alberta College of Art
Active in Canada since 1972

 Marin Marinov, restorer
Montreal, Quebec
b. 1949 Sofia, Bulgaria
Educated at School of Fine and
Applied Arts, Sofia, Bulgaria; National
Institute for Cultural Heritage, Sofia,
Bulgaria
Active in Canada since 1992

 Darrell Markewitz, blacksmith
Proton Station, Ontario
b. 1955 Guelph, Ontario
Educated at Ontario College of Art
Active in Canada since 1979

 Shelley Matthews-Blair
jewellery artist
Montreal, Quebec
b. 1962 Winnipeg, Manitoba
Educated at Alberta College of Art
Apprenticed under Ludwig
Nickel and Llyn Strelau
Active in Canada since 1991

 David McAleese, jeweller
Toronto, Ontario
b. 1947 Toronto, Ontario
Self-taught
Active in Canada since 1974

Colleen McCallum
Toronto, Ontario
b. 1951 Toronto, Ontario
Educated at Sheridan College School
of Design
Active in Canada 1974–85

Paul McClure, artist, jeweller
Toronto, Ontario
Educated at Escola Massana,
Barcelona, Spain; Nova Scotia College
of Art and Design
Active in Canada since 1986

Cathy McElroy, metalworker
Hornby Island, British Columbia
b. 1958 Tooela, Utah
Educated at Ontario College of Art
Active in Canada since 1981

Maggie McEwan, designer
Mississauga, Ontario
b. 1940 U.K.
Educated at Georgian College
Active in Canada since 1994

Van McKenzie, jeweller
Toronto, Ontario
b. 1957 Hamilton, Ontario
Educated at George Brown College
Active in Canada since 1988

 Ian Medland, silversmith
Cochrane, Alberta
b. 1952 Toronto, Ontario
Educated at Sheridan College
School of Design
Active in Canada since 1975

 Greg Merrall, teacher
Cookstown, Ontario
b. 1949 Toronto, Ontario
Educated at Loughborough
College of Art and Design, England;
Humber College
Active in Canada since 1970

Doreen G. Miller
Delta, British Columbia
b. 1933 Vancouver, British Columbia
Self-taught, with guidance from Edith
Heilman, Raymond, Washington
Active in Canada since 1962

Daniel Moisan
Saint-Hubert, Quebec
Educated at École de Joaillerie et des
Métaux d'Art de Montréal
Active in Canada since 1986

 Joan Steele Murray, jeweller
Georgeville, Quebec
b. 1919
Educated at School of Museum of Fine
Arts, Boston, Massachusetts
Active in Canada since 1973

 Simon Muscat, jeweller
Toronto, Ontario
b. Malta, 1955
Educated at Sheridan College School
of Design; George Brown College;
Ontario College of Art
Active in Canada since 1982

Lori Myers, jeweller
Toronto, Ontario
b. 1956 Regina, Saskatchewan
Educated at George Brown College;
Dalhousie University;
University of Toronto
Active in Canada since 1989

Kim Nagata, metalsmith
Calgary, Alberta
b. 1965 Calgary, Alberta
Educated at George Brown College
Active in Canada since 1989

LNI Ludwig Nickel, jeweller, enamellist
Winnipeg, Manitoba
b. 1935 Geiselwind, Bavaria
d. 1989 Winnipeg, Manitoba
Educated at Benedictine Monastery of
Muensterschwarzach under Adelman
Doelger; Journeyman certificate from
Chamber of Trade, District of
Wuerzburg. Regional winner of the
Practical Efficiency contest, Trades
Unions, District of Unterfranken,
Germany, 1953
Provincial winner, silversmith
trade in Bavaria, 1953
Active in Canada 1956–89

 Sandra Noble Goss, jeweller
Owen Sound, Ontario
b. 1946 Toronto, Ontario
Educated at Hornsey College of Art,
London, England; George Brown
College; York University
Active in Canada since 1973

 Harold T. O'Connor, goldsmith
Salida, Colorado
b. Utica, New York
Educated at University of New Mexico;
Instituto Allende, Mexico; National
Crafts School, Copenhagen; National
Arts School, Finland; Fachhochschule
fur Gestaltung, Pforzheim, Germany
Active in Canada 1971–75

JEO Jude Ortiz, artist, goldsmith
Echo Bay, Ontario
b. 1955
Educated at George Brown College;
Nova Scotia College of Art and Design
Active in Canada since 1980

Warren William Ottemiller
teaching master
Mississauga, Ontario
b. St. Marys, Pennsylvania
Educated at School for American
Craftsmen, Rochester, New York
Active in Canada since 1969

Tara Owen, jeweller
Calgary, Alberta
b. 1974 Calgary, Alberta
Educated at Alberta College of Art
Active in Canada since 1990

HP Helga Palko, goldsmith, enamellist
Spencerville, Ontario
b. 1928 Linz, Austria
Educated at California College of Arts
and Crafts, Oakland; Academy of Fine
Arts, University of Vienna
Active in Canada since 1955

Mark Peabody, designer, craftsman
Kingston, Ontario
b. 1966 St. Catharines, Ontario
Educated at Ontario College of Art
Active in Canada since 1988

 Betty J. Pehme, artist
Halfmoon Bay, British Columbia
b. 1938 Vancouver British Columbia
Studied at Vancouver School of Art;
West Vancouver Silversmiths
Association
Apprenticed under M. Chisholm,
Silversmith, West Vancouver,
British Columbia
Active in Canada since 1989

Joy Pennick, jeweller
Halifax, Nova Scotia
b. 1956 Toronto, Ontario
Educated at Nova Scotia College
of Art and Design; Sir Sandford
Fleming College
Active in Canada since 1990

 Alan Perkins, enamellist
Toronto, Ontario
b. 1915 Toronto, Ontario
Educated at Brookfield Craft School
Active in Canada since 1968

 Reeva Perkins, jeweller
Toronto, Ontario
b. 1917, d. 1994
Educated at George Brown College
Active in Canada from 1954–94

PETERSEN   Carl Poul Petersen, silversmith
Montreal, Quebec
b. 1895 Copenhagen, Denmark
d. 1977 Montreal, Quebec
Apprenticed at Georg Jensen
Silversmithy. With sons, Arno, John
Paul and Ole, ran C.P. Petersen &
Sons, 1944–79
Active in Canada 1929–77

 Frank X. Phillips, silversmith
Tenecape, Nova Scotia
b. 1921 Calgary, Alberta
Educated at Provincial Institute of
Technology and Art, Calgary; School
for American Craftsmen, Rochester,
New York. Apprenticed at Henry
Birks & Sons, Calgary
Active in Canada since 1946

Mary Kay Phipps
Sudbury, Ontario
b. 1941 Washington, DC
Educated at School of the Museum of
Fine Arts Boston;
Tufts University
Active in Canada 1965–74

 Virginie Planas, jeweller
Montreal, Quebec
b. 1967 Savigny sur Orge, France
Educated at L'École Nationale des
Beaux Arts, Paris

John Pocock, jeweller
Toronto, Ontario
b. 1912, d. 1975
Studied jewellery with
Nancy Meek Pocock
Active in Canada 1945–75

Mary Pocock, jeweller
Toronto, Ontario
b. Ottawa, Ontario
Educated at Carleton University;
Sheridan School of Design; Boston
University Program in Artisanry

Nancy Meek Pocock
Toronto, Ontario
Educated at Ontario College of Art
Active in Canada 1932–1975

 Josée Poulin, sculptor, jeweller
Montreal, Quebec
b. 1965 Montreal, Quebec
Educated at Saidye Bronfman Centre,
Montreal; École de Joaillerie et des
Métaux d'Art de Montréal; CEGEP,
Sherbrooke and Montreal, Quebec
Active in Canada since 1988

 Louise Aird Pringle, artist, jeweller
Regina, Saskatchewan
b. 1939 Coderre, Saskatchewan
Educated at University of
Saskatchewan; Banff School of Fine
Arts; Ottawa School of Art
Active in Canada since 1985

Laurel Putt, designer
Montreal, Quebec
b. 1949 Manitoba
Educated at Boston University
Program in Artisanry; Concordia
University

 Catherine Ramat, jeweller
St-Lambert, Quebec
b. 1957 Montreal, Quebec
Educated at Concordia University
Visual Arts Centre, Montreal
Active in Canada since 1984

Max Rapaport, artist
Outremont, Quebec
b. 1930 Montreal
Educated at École des Beaux-arts,
Montreal; University of Montreal;
McGill University
Took courses with Lois Betteridge and
Kye-yeon Son
Active in Canada since 1980

Heike Raschl(-Labrecque)
jewellery artist
Toronto, Ontario
b.1959 Stuttgart, Germany
Educated at Ontario College of Art;
George Brown College
Apprenticed under Armand
Brochard, Montreal
Active in Canada since 1981

Bill Reid, goldsmith
b. 1920, Victoria, British Columbia
Educated at Ryerson Technical
Institute, Toronto
Active in Canada since 1950

DJWR   David Reid
Toronto, Ontario
b. 1943 Dauphin, Manitoba
Educated at Central Technical
School, Toronto
Active in Canada since 1967

Margaret R. Reid, art teacher
Thornhill, Ontario
b. 1949 Port Huron, Michigan
Educated at Siena Heights College,
Adrian, Michigan
Active in Canada since 1984

Hokan Rudolph Renzius
pewtersmith, teacher
b. 1899 Malmo, Sweden
d. 1968 Newmarket, Ontario
Educated at Malmo Technical
University, with Just Anderson in
Copenhagen and Adolf von
Mayerhofer in Munich
Active in Canada 1923–63

 David Rice, jeweller
Winnipeg, Manitoba
b. 1947 Sioux Lookout, Ontario
Self-taught in jewellery
Active in Canada since 1970

Lisa Ridout, jeweller
Toronto, Ontario
b.1962 Oakville, Ontario
Educated at George Brown College
Active in Canada since 1992

PAM
RITCHIE   Pamela J. Ritchie, jeweller, teacher
Halifax, Nova Scotia
b. 1952 Amherst, Nova Scotia
Educated at Nova Scotia College
of Art and Design
Active in Canada 1975–79, 1982–

David Robertson, artist, blacksmith
Guelph, Ontario
b. 1964 Hamilton, Ontario
Educated at Sir Sanfred Fleming
College; University of Waterloo
Self-taught in smithing
Active in Canada since 1988

Winnifred D. Robertson
Surrey, British Columbia
b. 1930 Bonneyville, Alberta
Educated at Vancouver
Community College
Active in Canada since 1961

Graeme Robinson
Vancouver, British Columbia
b. England 1954
Educated at Hatfield Polytechnic,
England; Sheridan College
School of Design
Active in Canada since 1984

 James Robson, goldsmith, teacher
Toronto, Ontario
b. 1953 Saskatoon, Saskatoon
Educated at George Brown College;
Nova Scotia College of Art and
Design; University of Saskatchewan.
Active in Canada since 1973

Mila Rolicz
Toronto, Ontario
b. 1953 Montreal, Quebec
Educated at Dalhousie University;
University of British Columbia; George
Brown College
Active in Canada since 1990

 Fay Rooke, enamellist
b. 1934 Chatham, Ontario
Educated at Ontario College of Art
Member Royal Canadian Academy
Active in Canada since 1973

GMR   Glenda M. Rowley, metalsmith
Calgary, Alberta
b. 1963 Brandon, Manitoba
Educated at Alberta College of Art
Active in Canada since 1987

Brenda Roy, goldsmith
Everett, Ontario
b. 1957 Winnipeg, Manitoba
Educated at Georgian College;
University of Winnipeg;
University of Alberta
Active in Canada since 1991

Philip Salmon, designer
Toronto, Ontario
b. 1942 Manchester, England
Educated at Central Technical Art
School, Toronto
Active in Canada since 1976

Elvino Sauro
Toronto, Ontario
b. 1932 Niagara Falls, Ontario
Educated at University of Toronto;
Sussex University, England; Ryerson
Polytechnical University, Toronto;
George Brown College; Ontario
College of Art
Active since 1980

BSC Bozorth Scaife, jeweller
Mississauga, Ontario
b. Seattle, Washington
Educated at Syracuse University;
Central School of Arts and Crafts,
London; George Brown College
Apprenticed under Harry Goldin,
Syracuse, New York
Active in Canada since 1953

 Walter Schluep, jeweller
Montreal, Quebec
b. 1931 Costa Brava, Spain
Apprenticed under A. Siegel, Bienne,
Switzerland, and at the studios of
Albert Weber, Geneva, Switzerland,
and Gabriel Lucas, Montreal
Active in Canada since 1957

Karen Schmidt Humiski
Winnipeg, Manitoba
b. 1961 Winnipeg, Manitoba
Educated at University of Manitoba;
Sturgeon Creek Collegiate
Active in Canada since 1988

Karl Schutt, teacher
Ottawa, Ontario
b. 1942 Pembroke, Ontario
Educated at University of Manitoba;
University of British Columbia
Active in Canada since 1975

 Georges Schwartz, jeweller
Montreal, Quebec
b. 1929 Paris, France
Educated at Collège ARAGO, École
des Beaux-Arts, Paris
Apprenticed under F. Budai; H. Stossel
(Van Cleef & Arpels), Paris
Active in Canada since 1951

 Seagull Pewter
John Caraberis and Bonnie Bond)
(Pugwash, Nova Scotia
Self-taught in metal
Active in Canada since 1975

 Leslie Sheriff, jewellery designer
Toronto, Ontario
b.1958 Thunder Bay, Ontario
Educated at George Brown College
Active in Canada since 1979

Wendy Shingler, jeweller
Toronto, Ontario
b. 1938 Johannesburg, South Africa
Educated at St. Martin's School of Art,
London; University of Wisconsin;
George Brown College
Active in Canada since 1966

Mimi Shulman, jeweller
Toronto, Ontario
Educated at Sheridan College
School of Design;
Ontario College of Art
Active in Canada since 1970

Allyson Simmie
Iqaluit, Northwest Territories
b. 1967 Toronto, Ontario
Educated at University of British
Columbia; University of Ottawa; Nova
Scotia College of Art and Design
Active in Canada since 1988

 Tuen Sing (Stephen Fong), designer
Burnaby, British Columbia
b. 1959 Burma
Educated at Nova Scotia College of Art
and Design; Fachlochschule fur
Gestaltung, Pforzheim, Germany
Active in Canada since 1988

 Janice E. Smith, jewellery designer
Georgetown, Ontario
b. 1936 Montreal
Educated at Humber College; George
Brown College
Active in Canada since 1979

 Kim Snyder, jeweller
Kingston, Ontario
Educated at Ontario College of Art;
Sheridan College School of Design;
St. Lawrence College
Active in Canada since 1975

Kye-yeon Son, metalsmith
Quebec and Halifax, Nova Scotia
b. South Korea, 1957
Educated at Seoul National University;
Indiana University

Elisabeth Soppelsa, jeweller
Oakville, Ontario
b. Switzerland
Educated at Kunstgewerbeschule,
Zurich, Switzerland
Active in Canada since 1972

Jackie Spector, artist, goldsmith
Thornhill, Ontario
b. 1963 Montreal, Quebec
Educated at George Brown College;
Ontario College of Art; York University
Active in Canada since 1990

STACEY Harold Gordon Stacey
designer, craftsman
b. 1911 Montreal, Quebec
d. 1979 Toronto, Ontario
Educated at Northern Technical
School with Rudy Renzius; Handy &
Harman Silversmithing Workshop
Conference. Mostly self-taught
Active in Canada 1932–50,
1952–79

 Karl Heinz Stittgen, jeweller
Vancouver, British Columbia
b. 1930 Ludwigshafen, Germany
Apprenticed as finemechanic
Active in Canada since 1954

 Ellen Stock, goldsmith
Toronto, Ontario
b. Rheda, Germany
Educated at Sheridan College;
Humber, College;
George Brown College
Active in Canada since 1975

Susan Stopps, metalsmith
Toronto, Ontario
b. 1959 Wilmington, Delaware
Educated at George Brown College;
Ontario College of Art
Active in Canada since 1986

 Llyn L. Strelau
jewellery designer, goldsmith
Calgary, Alberta
b. 1955 Canwood, Saskatchewan
Self-taught
Active in Canada since 1973

Donald A. Stuart
gold and silversmith
Barrie, Ontario
b. 1944 Toronto, Ontario
Educated at Ontario College of Art;
School for American Crafts,
Rochester, New York
Member Royal Canadian Academy
Active in Canada since 1967

Barbara Stutman, designer
Montreal, Quebec
b. 1945 Montreal, Quebec
Educated at McGill University;
Museum of Fine Arts; Saidye
Bronfman Center; Concordia
University, Montreal
Active in Canada since 1982

Jack Sullivan
Toronto, Ontario
Taught at Ontario College of Art
1952–53, 1968–69

Yoshiko Sunahara, jeweller
Toronto, Ontario
b. Japan 1939
Educated at Musashino University of
Fine Arts, Tokyo
Active in Canada since 1984

Beni Sung, jewellery designer
Toronto, Ontario
b. Hong Kong
d. 1992 Toronto, Ontario
Educated at Ontario College of Art;
George Brown College
Active in Canada 1976–92

Louis-Jacques Suzor, jeweller
Montreal, Quebec
b. 1955, d. 1990
Educated at Collège Jean-de-Brebeuf;
École des Beaux-Arts de Montréal;
Ecole de Joaillerie et de Métaux d'Art
de Montréal.
Studied lapidary and gemmology with
Daniel Ungerson
Active in Canada 1976–90

MJDS David Swinson
gold and silversmith
Uxbridge, Ontario
b. 1952 Oshawa, Ontario
Educated at George Brown College
Active in Canada since 1978

Carl Frederick Torode
artist, goldsmith
Vancouver, British Columbia
b. 1960 Rhodesia
Educated at Kent Institute of Art and
Design, England; City and Guilds of
London Institute
Apprenticed at Highleys Jewellers,
Chatham, Kent, England
Active in Canada since 1985

Louis Tortell, jeweller
Toronto, Ontario
b. 1954 Malta
Educated at Royal University of Malta;
Sheridan College School of Design
Active in Canada since 1978

Jacques Troalen
designer, silversmith
Montreal, Quebec
b. 1949 Montreal, Quebec
Apprenticed under Ara Boyadjian,
Georges Schwartz, Ernest Blyth
and Frances Beck in London;
Sigurd Persson in Stockholm;
and Wulf Belard in Switzerland
Active in Canada since 1965

Todd Tyarm, artist
Vancouver, British Columbia
b. 1961 Kentucky
Educated at Antioch College, Ohio;
San Francisco Art Institute, California
Active in Canada since 1991

John Urban, jeweller
Low, Quebec
b. 1945 St. Paul, Minnesota
Self-taught in jewellery
Active in Canada 1974–94

Martina Urbas, artist
Vernon, British Columbia
b. 1959 Calgary, Alberta
Educated at Nova Scotia College of Art
and Design; David Thompson
University, Nelson, British Columbia
Apprenticed at Kaslo, British Columbia
Active in Canada 1983–87

Kenneth Grant Valen,
metalsmith, teacher
St. Andrews, New Brunswick
b. 1955 Mascouche, Quebec
Educated at Nova Scotia College
of Art and Design
Active in Canada since 1977

Adrienne van Riemskijk, jeweller
Mississauga, Ontario
b. 1942 the Netherlands
Educated at École des Arts
Décoratives et du Publicité, Brussels,
Belgium; St. Clare's College, Oxford;
Lambton College of Applied Arts and
Technology, Sarnia, Ontario; Humber
College
Active in Canada 1969–89

Tommia Vaughan-Jones
d.1993 Toronto, Ontario
Educated at Ontario College of Art;
School for American Craftsmen,
Rochester, New York; George Brown
College; Positano Art Workshop,
Positano, Italy;
Instituto Allende, Mexico
Evening courses in hollowware
with H. G. Stacey
Active in Canada 1954–93

Luci Veilleux, jeweller
Val Morin, Quebec
b. 1958 Ste. Rose Watford, Quebec
Educated at École de Joaillerie et de
Metaux d'Art de Montréal; CEGEP de
Ste-Foy, Quebec
Active in Canada since 1990

Ken Vickerson, teacher
Toronto, Ontario
b. 1958 Edmonton, Alberta
Educated at Alberta College of Art;
Banff School of Fine Arts; Northern
Alberta Institute of Technology,
Edmonton, Alberta
Active in Canada since 1981

Susan Wakefield, jeweller
Zephyr, Ontario
b. 1944 London, England
Educated at Montreal Museum School
of Fine Arts; Kent State University;
Sheridan College School of
Craft and Design
Active in Canada since 1980

Jan Waldorf, goldsmith
Oakville, Ontario
b. 1938 St. Lambert, Quebec
Educated at Sheridan College School
of Craft and Design; Atlin Art School
Active in Canada since 1970

Betty Walton
jewellery designer/manufacturer
Toronto, Ontario
b. 1948 Toronto, Ontario
Educated at George Brown College;
Ontario College of Art
Active in Canada since 1979

Donna Blakeman Welch
Winnipeg, Manitoba
b. 1953 Winnipeg, Manitoba
Educated at University of Manitoba

Wanda Wesolowski, designer
Elora, Ontario
b. 1933 Toronto, Ontario
Educated at George Brown College
Active in Canada since 1970

Richard J. Westwood
Hillsburgh, Ontario
b. Mottingham, Kent, U.K.
Self-taught
Active in Canada since 1993

Jacqueline White, goldsmith
Brantford, Ontario
b. 1971 Brantford, Ontario
Educated at Georgian College
Active in Canada since 1989

Alison Wiggins, studio jeweller
Toronto, Ontario
b. 1955 Toronto, Ontario
Apprenticed under David McAleese
Active in Canada since 1974

Lyn Wiggins, jeweller
Oakville, Ontario
b. 1941 Halifax, Nova Scotia
Educated at Sheridan College
School of Design
Active in Canada since 1974

Mark Wilson, designer
Etobicoke, Ontario
b. 1953 Toronto, Ontario
Educated at Ontario College of Art
Active in Canada since 1989

Catherine P. Windust, pewtersmith
Waterloo, Ontario
b. 1926 Woodstock, Ontario
Educated at University of Toronto;
University of Southampton, England
Studied pewter under Douglas
Shenstone
Active in Canada since 1969

Victoria Wollenberg, jeweller
Calgary, Alberta
b. 1967 Calgary, Alberta
Educated at Alberta College of Art

Mel Wolski, metalsmith
Barrie, Ontario
b. 1963 Calgary, Alberta
Educated at Alberta College of Art;
Nova Scotia College of Art and Design
Active in Canada since 1984

Simon Wroot, jeweller
b. 1950 England
Educated at Alberta College of Art;
Red Deer College; Lewton-
Brains/Fontans Centre for
Jewellery Studies
Active since 1990

Lucie and Barth Wttewaall
Sussex, New Brunswick
b. the Netherlands
Learned jewellery making from New
Brunswick Department of Handicrafts
Active in Canada 1954–87

Ann Wylie-Toal, designer
Flesherton, Ontario
b. 1955 Oakville, Ontario
Educated at University of Guelph
Active in Canada since 1987

Shang Yu, goldsmith
Vancouver, British Columbia
b. China
Active in Canada since 1981

132

anodizing   The creation of a porous skin on the surface of aluminum. This skin can then be coloured and sealed, creating a surface that is durable and non-conductive.

bezel   A thin band of metal that surrounds a stone and holds it in place.

brass   An alloy of copper and zinc.

bronze   An alloy of copper and tin.

brooch   From the French *broche* (meaning "spit" or "skewer"). A pin or clasp that can be fastened to a garment.

casting   The process of pouring or injecting molten metal into a mold to create a form.   **133**

chasing   The outlining or modeling of metal from the front side using various punches and a hammer. Used in conjunction with repoussé (pushing back) from the reverse side.

champlevé   A method of enamelling in which depressions are etched or engraved in metal and then filled with enamel.

cloisonné   A method of enamelling in which the enamel fills the spaces between an outline or design of wires that are soldered in place.

die forming   A technique using hard materials to impose a contour on sheet metal.

electroforming   A technique in which metal is electrolytically deposited onto a conductive matrix.

engraving   The cutting or incising of lines in the surface of metal with a sharp steel tool.

fabricated   Constructed by assembling parts or sections.

fibula   A decorative fastener used by ancient cultures to secure clothing. A forerunner to the kilt pin and safety pin.

filigree   Open ornamental work formed by soldering wires together.

forging   The process of shaping metal on an anvil or steel surface using a steel hammer. The jeweller usually employs cold forging methods, in which the metal is cold when hammered.

found object   Any item, natural or manufactured, that is picked up at random and used in an art piece.

fusing   The joining of pieces of metal by heating and melting without the use of solder.

granulation   An ancient process, using heat, in which small metal granules are attached to a metal surface without solder. Instead, at the point of contact, a type of diffusion bonding occurs, creating an alloy.

hollowware   Functional objects such as bowls and containers.

karat   (K, kt) The measure used to express the purity of gold, with 24-karat being the purest. An alloy of half pure gold and half other metals is 12 karats. (Distinguished from carat, a unit of measure used in the weighing of precious stones.)

keum-boo   A Korean technique for applying 24-karat gold to silver.

lamination   A process in which sheets of metal, often of different colour, are soldered together and then pressed or rolled out.

lapidary   of or relating to stones and the art of cutting them.

lapis-lazuli   An azure stone that often contains pyrites.

lost-wax casting   A process of casting that involves making a model in wax and investing it in a plaster or clay mold. When the mold is dry, the wax is melted out and the cavity is filled with molten metal.

marriage of metals   A process in which different metals are joined, often side by side, and then treated as one metal.

mokume gane   A Japanese technique in which layers of metal are laminated together and then cut into to expose inner striations that resemble woodgrain.

nickel silver   (German silver) A white metal alloy of approximately sixty-five percent copper, seventeen percent zinc and eighteen per cent nickel.

niello   A lustrous black inlay made of silver, lead, copper and sulfur.

niobium   A reactive metal the surface of which can be coloured in a wide range of bright colours through an electrolytic process.

patina   A surface colouration on metal achieved either naturally, through exposure to the atmosphere, or artificially, through the application of oxides, carbonates or sulfides.

photoetching A process in which photographic techniques are used to lay down a resist (coating) on a metal sheet, which is then acid etched.

piercing The cutting into or making of holes in metal, usually for a functional or decorative effect.

planishing The final smoothing of a metal surface by hammering.

plating An electrolytic process in which a thin layer of metal is deposited onto a conductive surface.

plique-à-jour A method of enamelling in which pierced openings in metal or openings in a filigree arrangement of wires are filled with translucent enamel, allowing light to pass through.

raising The forming of a hollow, three-dimensional shape from a flat sheet of metal by gradually bring up the sides in stages using a hammer against a steel stake.

repoussé The decorative process of pushing back metal with punches and a hammer from its reverse side after it has been chased down from the top side. The process is repeated as necessary until the desired definition is achieved.

reticulation A process in which metal is heat treated to create a textured surface of ridges and valleys.

rivet A piece of rod that goes through two pieces of metal and is then bulged at each end to hold the pieces together.

roller printing A technique in which a rolling mill is used to press a pattern or image into sheet metal

shakudo A Japanese copper alloy (between ninety-seven and seventy-five percent copper and three and twenty-five percent pure gold).

shibuichi A Japanese copper alloy (seventy-five percent copper and twenty-five percent silver).

spinning The process of turning sheet metal into a hollow form by forcing it against a metal or wood form on a rotating lathe.

stamping A technique in which steel punches are used to imprint an image or pattern on metal. Stamping also refers to the marking of quality and makers' marks.

titanium An extremely hard refractory metal the surface of which can be coloured using electrical current.

Anderson, Morna. *Metal Arts Guild of Nova Scotia,* 1951–1976. Halifax: 1976.

"Artists Should be Closer to Jeweller," *Canadian Jeweller*, Dec. 1962.

Ayre, Robert. "Creative Craftsmanship in Jewellery." *Canadian Art,* spring 1951.

Barber, Elizabeth Wayland. Women's Work: *The First 20,000 Years: Women, Cloth, and Society in Early Times.*
    New York: Norton and Co., 1994.

Barros, Anne. "Hero Kielman: Master Metalsmith." *Metalsmith,* winter 1984.

——"The Metal Arts Guild of Ontario." *Metalsmith,* spring 1984.

Bell, Andrew. "An Exhibition of Contemporary Canadian Arts," *Canadian Art*, summer 1950.

Brown, Raymond P. "Learning to Make Fine Jewellery." *Canadian Jeweller*, December, 1959.

Buchanan, Donald W. *First National Fine Crafts Exhibition*. Ottawa: National Gallery of Canada, 1957.

Canadian Craft Museum. *A Treasury of Canadian Craft*. Vancouver: 1992.

Canadian Crafts Council. *Artisan '78: The First National Travelling Exhibition of Contemporary Canadian Crafts.*
    Ottawa: Canadian Crafts Council, 1979.

Canadian Guild of Crafts (Ontario) and Ontario Science Centre. *Make (māk): Contemporary Crafts 1971*. Toronto: 1971.

Canadian Guild of Crafts (Ontario) and Royal Ontario Museum. *Craft Dimensions Canada*. Toronto: 1969.

"Canadian Metalsmith [Harold Stacey] Creates Unique Beauty." *Mayfair,* April 1951.

Canadian Museum of Civilization. *Masters of the Crafts*. Hull: 1989.

Conseil des metiers d'art du Quebec. "What is the Conseil des métiers d'art du Québec?" Quebec: 1994.

Crawford, Gail. "From Limited Means to Unlimited Success." *Craft News,* January–February 1994.

Cute, Virginia Wireman. "Contemporary American Silver." *Craft Horizons,* March–April 1952.

Duffek, Karen. *Bill Reid: Beyond the Essential Form*. Vancouver: University of British Columbia Press, 1986.

Eidelberg, Martin, ed. *Design: 1935–1965: What Modern Was*. New York:
    Le Musée des Arts Décoratifs de Montréal and Abrams, 1991.

Evans, James. "From Novitiate to Graduate: A History of Contemporary Canadian Jewellery." *Metalsmith*, spring 1985.

Hammel, Lisa. "On Her Mettle: Margret Craver." *American Craft*, June–July 1991.

Hanks, Carole. "A Closer Look." *Metalsmith*, winter 1988.

Herman, Lloyd. *Brilliant Stories: American Narrative Jewelry*. Washington DC: International Sculpture Center, 1994.

Hughes, Graham. *Modern Jewelry*. New York: Crown Publishers, 1963.

Ignatieff, Helen. "Ontario Silversmiths." *Canadian Antiques Collector,* May 1971.

Illingworth Kerr Gallery. *Jackie Anderson*. Calgary: 1993.

Inglis, Stephen, "The Island of Craft . . . and an Outgoing Tide." *Ontario Craft*, Fall 1987.

Kaplan, Enid. "Galerie Jocelyne Gobeil, Montreal, Canada." *Metalsmith*, winter 1992.

Lacroix, Marie-Josée. "Gilles Beaugrand: Soixante Ans d'Orfèvrerie." *Le Bel Âge*, May 1992.

Larochelle-Roy, Lise. *L'Émail au Québec*. Ville Saint-Laurent: Musée d'Art de Saint-Laurent, 1990.

Leitch, Adelaide. "The Silversmiths of Sussex." *Canadian Geographic Journal*, June 1958.

Lesser, Gloria. "Carl Poul Petersen: Master Danish-Canadian Silversmith." *Material History Review*, spring 1996.

Lucie-Smith, Edward. *American Craft Today: Poetry of the Physical*. New York: American Craft Museum, 1986.

Massey, Hart. *The Craftsman's Way*. Toronto: University of Toronto Press, 1981.

Matzdorf, Kurt. *The Founding Masters*. Saratoga Springs, N.Y.: Schick Art Gallery and Skidmore College, 1988.

Mays, John Bentley. "Comment." *American Craft*, December 1985.

McGinnis, Graham. *Canadian Art*. Toronto: Macmillan, 1950.

Morton, Philip. *Contemporary Jewelry*. Holt, Rinehart and Winston, 1970.

Olympic Arts Festival. *Restless Legacies: Contemporary Craft Practice in Canada*. Calgary: 1988.

Ontario Craft Foundation Newsletter. November 1968.

Payne, Anne. "People of the Arts." *Arts West*, No. 4, Vol. 2, 1977.

Pulos, Arthur J. "Metalsmithing in the 1940s and 1950s: A Personal Recollection." *Metalsmith*, spring 1983.

Regis College. *Canadian Religious Art Today*. Willowdale: 1966.

Reid, Bill. "The Art: An Appreciation." *Arts of the Raven*. Vancouver: Vancouver Art Gallery, 1967.

Rose, Muriel. "Crafts in Contemporary Life." *Canadian Art*, October–November 1943.

Scott, Charles H. "New Tides in West Coast Art." *Canadian Art*, December, 1949.

Shenstone, Douglas A. *For the Love of Pewter*. Toronto: 1990.

Stacey, Robert. "Stacey Sterling." *Metalsmith*, spring 1985.

Stefanutti, Erika Ayala and Gary S. Griffin. "Remaking Material." *Metalsmith,* summer 1994.

Stittgen, Karl. "Jewellers are Missing the 'Custom Design' Boat." *Canadian Jeweller*, June 1961.

The Creative Jewellers Guild of B.C.: *A Short History*. Richmond: 1994.

Vancouver Art Gallery. *Bill Reid: A Retrospective Exhibition*. 1974.

Vancouver International Festival. *The Arts in French Canada*. Vancouver Art Gallery, 1959.

Williamson, Moncrieff. *Canadian Fine Crafts: An Exhibition collected for the Canadian Government Pavilion*. Ottawa: Queen's Printer, 1967.

Wyman, Max. *Toni Cavelti: A Jewellers Life*. Vancouver: Douglas and McIntyre, 1996.

140

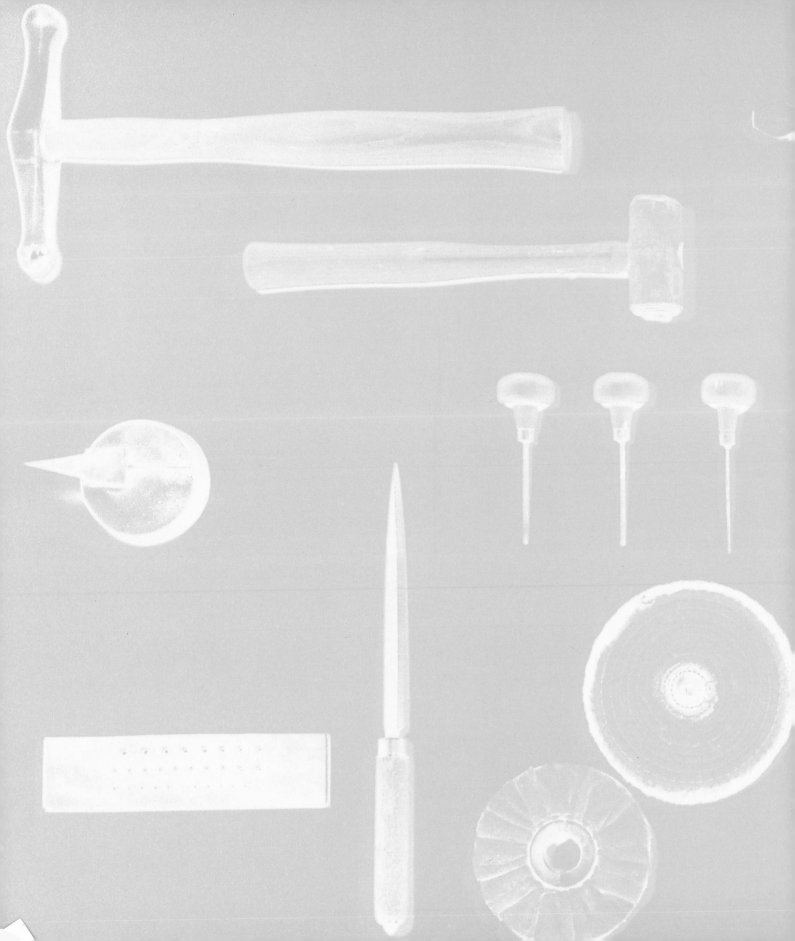